THE
Scales of Training
WORKBOOK

THE
Scales of Training
WORKBOOK

Claire Lilley

▶ J. A. Allen

First published in Great Britain 2010 by J.A. Allen, an imprint of
The Crowood Press Ltd, Ramsbury, Marlborough, Wiltshire SN8 2HR

enquiries@crowood.com

www.crowood.com

This impression 2020

ISBN 978 0 85131 970 4

British Library Cataloguing-in-Publication Data
A catalogue record for this book is available from the British Library.

The right of Claire Lilley to be identified as author of this work has been asserted by her
in accordance with the Copyright, Designs and Patents Act 1988.

Disclaimer of Liability
The author and publisher shall have neither liability nor responsibility to any person or entity with respect to any loss or damage caused or alleged to be caused directly or indirectly by the information contained in this book. While the book is as accurate as the author can make it, there may be errors, omissions, and inaccuracies.

Design by Judy Linard
Edited by Jane Lake

Printed and bound in India by Replika Press Pvt. Ltd.

This book is dedicated to **Carina Amadeus 1993–2009**

Amadeus was a very special horse who taught me more than anyone about the scales of training. Not an easy horse to ride, he had a wicked sense of humour and would delight in putting my skills to the test every day. If I got it 'right', he would work perfectly but if I made mistakes, he would certainly let me know! Riding a horse who was so clever helped me to discover the right and wrong ways to train.

Amadeus played a large part in the evolvement of this book. I hope I have done him justice and passed on the knowledge I acquired during our fourteen years together.

Contents

2 Suppleness (Looseness – *Losgelassenheit*)   61

3 Contact (*Anlehnung*)   86

Acknowledgements

I would like to thank all the riders – Rachel Waine, Louise Holden, Jo Ingram, Pernilla Swedérus, Manuela Bellows, Catherine Petchey – and their horses who have been kind enough to let me trail after them with a camera, and my husband Dougald for his photography. My thanks also to Lesley Gowers, Jane Lake and Judy Linard of J. A. Allen for their hard work in putting this book together.

Foreword

The scales of training refer to the basic schooling of every horse, at all levels from novice upwards. If the scales are not correct at novice level, then it is unlikely that horse and rider will progress to advanced levels and be able to maintain a consistent level of achievement.

Training horses takes dedication, time and understanding. The scales of training give the rider a logical system to follow that allows the horse to develop both physically and mentally over a period of time.

This book explains what the scales are and how to use them, whether the rider wishes to concentrate on dressage, jumping or eventing: they are not exclusive to the dressage horse. It includes exercises for both dressage and jumping to develop the horse's natural ability and to improve the rider's understanding of the horse's educational needs.

Ingrid Klimke

Rhythm – Suppleness – Contact – Impulsion – Straightness – Collection

The 'scales of training' are the foundations on which the schooling of every horse should be based, whether the rider wishes to concentrate on dressage, jumping or eventing, and are essential to any horse's physical and mental development at all levels from novice upwards. The scales must be established correctly at novice level otherwise progression to advanced levels is hampered and maintaining a steady level of achievement will not be possible. The scales work in a chronological sequence and are inter-related; they all relate to every stage of the horse's training to some degree.

In dressage competitions the scales are used at all levels to check if a horse's way of going is correct, but they are also essential for jumping. A balanced, obedient horse who is supple and straight will develop a good jumping technique and go much further in his career and be easier and more pleasurable to ride than a horse who is poorly trained (see Figure I.1).

Figure I.1 *A correctly trained horse is a pleasure to ride and a joy to watch! The horse should be happy in his work and there should be harmony between horse and rider. Eight-year-old Trakehner gelding Heinrich (Broomdowns Donaupasquale) and I demonstrate a good, well-balanced trot.*

History of the Scales of Training and their Evolvement

The scales of training are the components of a progressive training system, which evolved from the teaching of the great riding masters of Italy, France and Germany. German riders are very successful in dressage and jumping as a result of their systematic approach to training.

The scales are rooted in the traditions of the Spanish Riding School, in particular the teachings of the Austrian riding master Max von Weyrother, who was greatly influenced by the French master, de la Guérinière. Other influential horsemen were German master, Seeger, who studied under Max von Weyrother, Gustav Steinbrecht and Italian master, Caprilli, who invented the forward seat for jumping.

Gustav Steinbrecht (1808–1885), one of the great German trainers, was fanatical about forming the outline of the horse in the right way. He was of the opinion that the horse should be trained without haste, and that the exercises should: 'All follow one another in such a way that the preceding exercise always constitutes a secure basis for the next one. Violations of this rule will always exert payment later on; not only by a triple loss of time but very frequently by resistances, which for a long time if not forever interfere with the relationship between horse and rider.'

The scales of training were developed for the German cavalry school in Hanover and the rules were first laid down in 1912. They were set in their present form in the 1950s.

How the six scales of training work together

Rhythm (*Takt*) (**1**) means regular steps in the horse's gaits: walk, trot, and canter. Establishing a good rhythm enables the horse to relax. A relaxed horse with a good rhythm develops **suppleness** (*Losgelassenheit*) (**2**). A loose (supple) horse is able to work through his back (*Durchlässigkeit*) and happily accept a soft and even rein **contact** (*Anlehnung*) (**3**). Working into the contact enables the horse to develop power and strength, i.e. **impulsion** (*Schwung*) (**4**). A horse that can move slowly and powerfully into a soft elastic contact, becomes **straightened** (*Geraderichten*) (**5**) and develops the strength to take weight on his hindquarters, improving his balance and enabling him to work in **collection** (*Versammlung*) (**6**).

Following the scales of training is the only way to ensure that your horse works on the bit with the poll the highest point in a correct outline with the nose vertical, or just in front of the vertical, with his back lifted and the hind legs under the body.

A horse should become 'round' as a result of correct training and because it is a result of the right exercises performed in the correct order for the individual horse. All the scales interrelate, and priorities may change should the horse have a particular problem which needs to be addressed. For example, a horse that is not straight (scale 5) will find it difficult to work in a rhythm (scale 1), so the horse needs straightening exercises before rhythm exercises. An unbalanced horse will be irregular in its rhythm, so the priority would be to teach the horse to take weight behind (the early stage of collection, scale 6) before a rhythm can be established. The scales interrelate to such an extent that they all have a bearing on every other scale.

The rider's aids and position and the horse's way of going are covered in the book as they crop up in each chapter because if these factors are not correct, the exercises cannot be executed properly.

Developing a Horse Correctly

These days, many trainers dismiss the art of lungeing and in-hand work as unnecessary, but these play an important part in the horse's education. It is very helpful for the rider to assess their horse from the ground; actually seeing how the horse looks when he is working gives the rider great insight into the ridden training that is required. Issues that arise in ridden work can often be solved from the ground with less stress for both horse and rider than trying to 'ride through it'. Lungeing and in-hand work are used in this book where appropriate.

Today, it is also all too common to see horses who have been trained incorrectly by riders looking for a quick fix. Pulling the horse's neck into a 'round outline' so that the horse is overbent and fiddling with the bit to create 'submission' causes tension throughout the horse's back and renders the hind legs useless at taking weight. (See Figures I.2a and b)

Many physical problems result from this attitude, and cost the owner a lot of money in vets'

Figures I.2a and b *Good outlines being demonstrated in a)* (right top) *by Amadeus and me: medium trot, and in b)* (right bottom) *by Manuela Bellows and her four-year-old Andalusian gelding, Lugareñ XII: walk.*

fees, the outcome of which may be that the horse is no longer physically or mentally able to do the job. This kind of rider then buys another horse, and does the same thing all over again. Many potentially wonderful horses are ruined by such an attitude.

Taking one horse from the beginning of his training through to the higher levels is extremely satisfying, and a real partnership is developed. Understanding and following the scales is the way of 'body-building' the horse progressively over several years. Not all horses and their riders will have the physical or mental attributes to reach the higher echelons of the Olympics, but it is great fun trying! Whatever your field of interest, be it playing polo, hacking at the weekend, western riding, and so on, the horse will benefit from developing progressively over time.

Muscles to look for if your horse is working correctly

The top two muscles of the neck should be seen clearly and the muscles under the neck should be relaxed, as should the poll. The neck should be evenly muscled along its length. The horse should be mouthing the bit quietly. The belly muscles should be toned and supporting the spine from underneath and the haunches should be well muscled with the pelvis tucked under. The loins should be lifted. The hind and forelegs should be muscled evenly. (See Figures I.3a and b)

Figures I.3a and b *a)* (above left) *Louise Holden riding Arabian gelding Psalute. This young horse's muscles are not yet fully developed. b)* (above right) *In contrast, this horse shows well-developed musculature and demonstrates correct bend on a circle, Pernilla Swedérus riding Andalusian stallion Berilio.*

This musculature applies just as much to the jumping horse as the dressage horse because a jumping horse has to bascule over a fence and round his back in order to clear the fence.

An incorrectly muscled horse, on the other hand, will have little or no back muscle covering the spine, and dipped loins. He will appear to be upside down. The haunches will appear weak and the thigh muscles will be underdeveloped. The forelimbs will be more muscled as they are taking more weight than the hind legs (on the forehand). The hind legs will be 'out behind' and not under the haunches and the horse will be hollow-backed (see Figure I.4). The horse will have a 'beer belly' when the belly muscles are

Figure I.4 *If a horse is not asked to step under behind and engage the hind legs, the hind legs will move stiffly and not flex at the joints, and he will be hollow-backed.*

slack and neither supporting the back from underneath nor bringing the hind legs under the body (tucking the pelvis).

A horse who is thicker under the neck than on the top line of the neck will be tight at the poll and tense through the jaw, resisting the bit. There will be a dip in the muscles just in front of the withers. The underneath neck muscle will be prominent. A horse who does not flex through the poll will have thickened muscles at the head end of the neck; this will cause the horse difficulty in relaxing the jaw, and he will tend to avoid the contact and flexing at the poll by lowering his head. These muscles develop over time if the horse is continually worked 'deep' or bitted too strongly. If a horse does not work through from behind sufficiently he could drop his poll and come behind the bit. Also, if a rider restricts a horse too much with the rein aids, or the horse avoids proper contact with the bit, he can become overbent; if a horse is habitually ridden overbent vertebrae can be damaged. (See Figures I.5a–e)

Figures I.5a–e *a) The muscle under the neck is overdeveloped and the back is tense behind the saddle.*
b) Not flexing through the poll has caused this horse to be overbent and he is resisting the strong contact.
c) This horse is not working 'through his back' to the contact and is avoiding the contact by dropping the
poll. He is also on his forehand but d) shows the same horse now working correctly on the bit. e) The arrow
on this photograph indicates where the neck has been damaged previously by the horse being ridden
consistently overbent, although this photo shows that after retraining he is in a correct outline with the nose
vertical and the poll the highest point. See Figure 3.8a on page 115 to see the same horse working with
better-developed neck muscles several months later.

A horse who has not been produced in the right way will not be able to work effectively and comfortably. Such a horse will have difficulty gaining good marks in a dressage test, and probably knock down, or refuse at, more fences than he clears! Whatever his job, the horse should appear to work in a rounded outline (on the bit), swing through his back and be in self-carriage. This is the ultimate goal of the scales of training. (See Figure I.6)

Figure I.6 *Well-presented piaffe is something you can aspire to if you aim to produce your horse properly through the scales of training.*

1 Rhythm (*Takt*)

> **What is rhythm?**
> Rhythm is the regularity of the gait, rather like the ticking of a clock.

Takt is the German word for rhythm, which denotes the regularity of the steps in the horse's gaits. Rhythm is most commonly listed as the first subject in the scales of training, and Suppleness as the second. But here is an interesting question: does a horse working in a rhythm become supple (loose) or does a loose horse work in a rhythm? It is possible (and commonly seen in dressage competitions) for a tense horse to work in a rhythm, resulting in so-called flashy gaits. When researching this book I found that Rhythm was placed second in the scales of training by the older German school of horsemanship with Suppleness (looseness) taking pole position, which does seem more logical. Surely it is more correct, and far better for the horse's well-being, to establish looseness as a priority over showy, tense strides? More recently veterinary surgeon Gerd Heuschmann, in his book *Tug of War*, says, 'In my opinion, even experienced trainers would benefit from reassessing the order and interdependence of the first two elements on the Training Scale. I believe, for example, that rhythm is impossible to achieve without a fundamental degree of looseness.'

There are two questions that lead on from this. Does a horse working in a rhythm become relaxed? Does a relaxed horse work in a rhythm? Establishing a rhythm in the gaits certainly helps the horse to relax and to settle into his work. The horse may be having an off day, be a bit spooky and not listen to the rider's aids. If the rider then takes control and influences the horse with a firmer position and clearer, firmer aids, then the horse can pick up the required rhythm from the rider's seat. (See page 23) For instance, if the horse is taking short, tense steps in the walk, the rider can take over the horse's back movement and increase the length of the stride but this has to be done tactfully and with feeling rather than force.

Defining Rhythm

A relaxed horse will work in a rhythm. A horse who is suffering any form of pain, physical problem or discomfort, such as lameness or backache, will be tense to some degree and consequently will not work in a rhythm. A comfortable horse will be able to relax and so relaxation is an indicator of general well-being in the horse.

Rhythm is most commonly spoilt by tension in the rider or the horse, when either becomes anxious. Sitting quietly in the saddle and letting the horse move underneath you is, in my opinion, the most important yet the most difficult aspect of riding to master. A tense rider creates anxiety in the horse, which can have an adverse effect on rhythm however talented the horse is. Even the most flowing, natural gaits can be changed into a shuffling mess by a tense rider.

Tension or lameness affect all horses whatever breed or type they are, but the type of gait has nothing to do with the quality of the rhythm, and the difference in stride length should not affect a horse's ability to work in a rhythm. A Thoroughbred has a different gait from that of a Shetland pony, but they can both work in a rhythm and it is important that the breed of the horse must not influence the onlooker when assessing rhythm.

A fit, healthy horse free in the field will move in rhythm in all gaits, even when excited. When rhythm is affected by lameness or injury, stiffness or pain, professional advice should be sought. Ill-fitting tack, poor shoeing and sharp teeth can all have an effect on the horse's well-being and thus his ability to work in relaxed, rhythmic gaits.

Rhythm applies to *all* gaits and movements, not just to the basic gaits of walk, trot and canter, but also to the gallop, advanced movements such as piaffe, passage and tempi changes in canter, specialist gaits like the Spanish walk or the tølt of the Icelandic pony, the naturally high knee action of a Hackney or Welsh Cob, or the floating steps of an Arab. Lateral work requires regularity and dressage movements should appear smooth and effortless, whether performed with the longer sweeping steps of the Warmblood, or the higher, staccato steps of the Iberian horse – which can be misconstrued as tension or stiffness by the untrained eye.

A jumping horse needs to develop rhythm in his canter particularly to cope with the demands of the jumping course. It is far less stressful, both mentally and physically, for the horse to jump a round of jumps in a rhythm than to stop/start around the course because the rider has not planned the turns in the course properly or counted the strides where appropriate between related fences. Working uphill and downhill affects the stride and balance of the horse but it should not affect the rhythm.

The event horse who is physically fit and mentally prepared for his work is able to go round a cross-country course in a rhythm, whether galloping between fences, or collecting in preparation for the next obstacle on level or undulating ground.

Rhythm can be adversely affected by a lack of confidence on either the part of the horse or the rider. The two members of the partnership may not trust each other, or the horse may not be confident on the ground surface. Working on slippery or uneven surfaces with nasty surprises such as pot holes or muddy patches or frozen ground can certainly affect rhythm. A good surface such as a well-designed arena or a level field can make a huge difference to how a horse moves rhythmically.

 ## The Rider's Influence on Rhythm

Horses naturally move in rhythmic gaits but these can be messed up so easily by the rider. It does help the horse's quality of movement in his gaits if the rider has a sense of rhythm. One of the best ways of establishing this is to ride to music. Even just putting the radio on and riding along to different tracks can help. (See my book *Dressage to Music* – J.A. Allen.)

Many riders ask a horse to go forwards by pushing with the seat. This causes the horse's back muscles to tighten and contract, hollowing the back, which restricts the movement of the horse and the regularity of the steps. The pushing seat is often combined with frantic leg aids randomly applied which are, more often than not, ignored or misunderstood by the horse, rendering the aids ineffective. These aids will push the horse out of his rhythm, causing him to speed up as he tries to run away from the harsh seat. The rider then becomes stressed and resorts to strong rein aids to hold the horse together. Alternatively a horse may become sluggish and slow as he tightens his back against the discomfort, in which case the rider then resorts to excessive whip and/or spurs to keep the horse going. The solution to the problem is, however, quite simple: sit quietly and allow the horse to relax his back so that he is able to respond to the aids, and work in a

Figure 1.1 *I show a balanced seat on Dangerous Liaison (Norman) a six-year-old Hanoverian/Thoroughbred gelding by Demonstrator. The reins are deliberately long to demonstrate how a rider should be able to maintain her position without relying on them for support. Sitting in the middle of the horse and allowing him to work correctly through his back is essential for your horse to work in a rhythm underneath you. I could be looking up a bit more!*

rhythm. (This also applies to impulsion where the seat has to allow forwardness.) This endorses the opinion that Looseness (which requires relaxation) should come before Rhythm in the scales.

In order to allow a horse to keep his rhythm and to use his back effectively, the rider must have a correct, balanced seat. The best way to acquire and/or improve your seat is on a trained horse on the lunge, working without reins and, later, also without stirrups. You need to sit up tall in the saddle using your trunk muscles to support your upper body. Slack stomach muscles result in the rider sitting heavily and wriggling about like a sack of rats and this will not give anyone a balanced seat! When you are sitting in balance on a chair, you do not have to move at all as the chair is static. A horse, however, is a moving creature, and so to be properly balanced on a horse, the movement of your hips and spine should be synchronised with the horse's back movement, giving the appearance of being completely at one with your horse; a picture of unity. (See Figure 1.1)

A correct, balanced seat is *only* achieved by sitting as tall as you can in the saddle with toned stomach and back muscles. Your chest and ribs should be lifted, and your shoulders back and down. Let your legs stretch down with your heels in a vertical line with your hips. Your shoulders should also be in line with your hips, as they should be when you are standing upright on the ground – you should not be leaning either backwards or forwards. Keep your weight on the balls of your feet in the stirrups, and allow your heel to 'sink' from a softly flexed ankle. Ramming the heels down can cause you to lean backwards and push the lower leg forwards, so it is not in an effective position against the horse's belly. Lifting the heel causes the lower leg to swing too far back which would tip you too far forwards in the saddle. Ideally you should sit with your hips upright and feel as though you are being stretched upwards and downwards at the same time! This helps you to isolate and use your lumbar and abdominal muscles which control your hips, and control of your hips should enable

Figure 1.2 *A correct, balanced seat with the upper body upright. My legs are down and in contact with the horse's sides; my hands are carried just above the withers with my elbows against my body, and I am looking forwards between the horse's ears. A rider must be able to control their own body in order to give clear and subtle aids to the horse.*

you to follow the horse's back movement with your seat bones (base of your pelvis). Think in terms of 'walking seat bones', 'trotting seat bones', or 'canter seat bones'; nothing else should wiggle about.

When this is mastered, you can help a horse to develop a better rhythm by influencing the stride with the pelvis as required. The seat bones are the base of the pelvis, and the right and left hip bones at the top of the pelvis. (See Figure 1.2)

Extending the stride

Should a rider wish to lengthen the horse's stride in the walk, a 'bigger' walk, trot or canter movement is made with the seat bones. The back should swing with the horse's back. The calves ask the horse to maintain the forwards movement, and the thighs and knees soften slightly to allow the horse to take bigger steps.

Collecting the stride

To collect the stride, a 'smaller' walk, trot or canter movement is made with the seat bones. Also, the rider must sit as tall as possible, firming up the muscle tone around the trunk and closing the legs onto the horse to 'hold' the gait, so that the steps cover less ground but become more elevated. I often describe this feeling as 'picking the horse up around the ribs'. The seat muscles must remain soft and no extra pressure must be put onto the horse's back, otherwise he cannot lift his back under the rider. In other words, if a rider presses down on the saddle, the horse cannot tuck his pelvis under and lift his loins, and he does not, therefore, take weight behind – a necessary function of collection (see Collection, page 174).

The legs should lie quietly against the horse and have sufficient muscle tone to keep them in place; the lower legs giving subtle nudges in sync with the horse's belly movement, i.e. giving a nudge when it feels natural to do so within the rhythm of the horse's gait.

The rein aids should also be subtle. Strong aids will disrupt the rhythm of the gait, as will the anticipation of a jab in the mouth. Only a horse working into a relaxed, steady contact will work with regularity (see Contact, page 86).

 ## Rhythm in Jumping

Position

Maintaining rhythm is paramount to successful jumping. A secure jumping seat is essential for remaining in rhythm with the horse's stride over obstacles, and on the ground between a series of jumps. It also enables a rider to remain in balance with the horse when jumping obstacles and when travelling at speed, and gives security in the saddle should anything untoward happen. When approaching an obstacle you should be sitting as you would in the dressage seat, sitting upright on your seat bones with your seat in contact with the saddle and with your upper body upright or very slightly in front of the vertical. It is advisable to shorten your stirrups three or four holes to allow your thighs to lie snugly against the saddle, in front of the upper body, with the knees supported by the knee rolls of the jumping saddle. This is an extremely efficient and secure position, especially when your weight is on the balls of your feet with the heels deeply flexed. It is important to develop the ability to let your weight come down through the whole leg so as not to risk losing a stirrup by inadvertently raising the knee or heel. Your lower leg should remain underneath you at all times.

When jumping, the momentum of the horse's bascule will cause you to fold forward voluntarily, but tension in your hips will hinder the jump and could result in you being left behind or the horse hollowing his back and dropping his hind legs. With a secure jumping seat, you should be able to remain in rhythm

Figure 1.3 *Jo Ingram on twelve-year-old Dutch Warmblood Trevor showing a secure, balanced jumping seat. Her weight is in her stirrups with her lower legs from the knee down secure against Trevor's sides. Her seat is slightly raised out of the saddle, but she remains close to Trevor's back so as not to disturb him in the air. Her spine is in line with his back and her hands are forwards, allowing him to fully stretch his neck forwards for balance.*

with the horse's canter stride and to keep the rein contact elastic, allowing the horse to take off, bascule, and land while maintaining a light contact with the bit throughout (see Contact, page 86).

Try to avoid becoming too floppy as this causes the upper body to become very unstable and you risk being thrown off balance by the horse and either dropping the contact altogether, or pulling the horse in the mouth. In a correct jumping position, with a secure lower leg, you will remain in balance should the horse hesitate or attempt to refuse and be able to ride him effectively in adverse situations. (See Figures 1.3 and 1.4a–d)

Figures 1.4a–d *This sequence shows Catherine Petchey with six-year-old Thoroughbred gelding Spartan Archer in action across country over a drop fence. Catherine's lower leg remains in a secure position throughout ensuring that she stays in balance with Archie as he jumps. She gives with the reins to allow him to fully use his neck for balance but retains just enough contact in readiness for the get-away after the fence so that they can gallop on to the next obstacle without disturbing the rhythm of the stride.*

Rhythm in the Gaits

Walk

The walk has four beats and no period of suspension as the horse picks up one foot at a time. The sequence of footfalls in the walk starts with a hind leg, in this case the left hind:

- left hind
- left fore
- right hind
- right fore.

As you can see, the hind leg is followed by the front leg on the same side (see Figures 1.5a–d). A horse who is tense through his back, or not relaxed into the contact, can tend to pace, i.e. the legs on the same side are moved together which

Figures 1.5a–d
Lipizzaner/ Thoroughbred gelding Amadeus and I show the sequence of legs in the walk: left hind, left fore, right hind, right fore. There is no period of suspension and so the walk is said to have no impulsion as such, but it should be active. The walk shown here is collected, showing a short stride, but it could have a bit more activity with the horse's feet lifting a little higher off the ground.

means that the walk loses the four-beat rhythm and becomes a two-beat gait. Tension in the walk can also result in jogging, a two-beat gait, which is in effect a trot.

There are four types of walk.

Collected walk

In collected walk a horse takes short, elevated steps. He covers less ground than in medium walk, but he should pick his feet up clearly and with activity, i.e. not dragging his toes and scuffing the ground. He should be correctly on the bit, with the poll the highest point, and the nose vertical to the ground.

Medium walk

Medium walk is the horse's 'normal' walk on the bit. The steps are bigger and the horse covers more ground than in collected walk. The neck should be arched forwards into a steady contact.

Free walk

In free walk, the horse should be exactly that: free with no rein contact. In the British Dressage rule book, the free walk is described as 'a pace of relaxation in which the horse is allowed complete freedom to lower and stretch out his head and neck.' However, in dressage tests, the movement is often described as 'a free walk on a long rein'. I don't see how a walk can be 'free' if it is on a long rein but feel that a true free walk would be on a loose rein.

In free walk, the horse should take ground-covering steps which at least track up or even overtrack (see pages 32 and 33).

Extended walk

In extended walk, the horse takes bigger steps than in medium walk. In essence, extended walk is free walk on a contact. The horse should lengthen his frame, i.e. be allowed to reach forwards to the bit by the rider's hands 'offering the bridle forwards', which allows the horse to walk 'through his whole body'.

Iberian breeds are adept at performing **Spanish walk**, when the forelegs are raised, almost to chest height, when they step forwards, but other breeds can be trained to do this. Although it is not an official movement in FEI dressage tests, it can be useful for loosening up the horse's shoulders and elevating the forehand! This must also be in a four-beat rhythm, and problems arise with the purity of the walk if the trainer is not diligent in maintaining this.

Trot

The trot is a two-beat gait with the horse moving his legs in diagonal pairs. There is a period of suspension between each diagonal pair hitting the ground when all four feet are off the ground. (See Figure 1.6)

Figure 1.6 This young Andalusian gelding shows a clear diagonal pair in the trot. He is tracking up because his hind feet are stepping into the prints of his front feet. On a circle, the inside pair of feet will appear to touch.

Collected trot

Collected trot has short, elevated steps. The horse should be in an 'uphill' position, i.e. the poll should be the highest point, the haunches lowered, and the horse should appear light with a raised forehand. The lifted forehand enables the horse to perform school movements, such as lateral work, with ease. (See Figure 1.13a, page 42)

Working trot

Working trot is the horse's 'normal' trot, i.e. a trot rhythm and tempo that he finds easy to maintain and that allows him to relax and work in balance. This trot should be established before attempting any degree of collection or lengthening of the strides. (See Figure 1.13b, page 42)

Medium trot

Medium trot comes between working and extended trot. The horse lengthens his stride and frame making a 'bigger' version of working trot, maintaining balance and energy with more push off the ground. The trot should 'come out through the shoulder' more than in working trot, but remember that the hind and front legs must work as matching pairs; trailing hind legs and 'flashy' front legs are not acceptable. (See Figure 1.13c page 42)

Extended trot

In extended trot, the horse lengthens his stride as much as he can while remaining in balance, and lengthens his frame, putting his nose just in front of the vertical, while remaining on an elastic contact. The rider should 'push the bridle forwards' to help the horse to reach forwards with his shoulders to match the push coming from the hind legs. The activity of fore and hind legs should be equal. Extended trot is a bigger and more dramatic version of a medium trot.

Canter

The canter is a three-beat gait with a moment of suspension, and so in effect the canter has a four-time beat. This is particularly noticeable when riding to music.

The leg sequence for **left canter** is:

- right hind
- right fore and left hind together (diagonal pair)
- left fore (leading leg); this leg steps onto the ground while the diagonal pair is still on the ground, so all three legs are on the ground together for a moment
- period of suspension (all four feet off the ground) when the outside hind leg swings forwards in readiness for the next canter stride.

The leg sequence for **right canter** is:

- left hind
- left fore and right hind (diagonal pair)
- right fore (leading leg); this leg steps onto the ground while the diagonal pair is still on the ground, so all three legs are on the ground together for a moment
- period of suspension (all four feet off the ground) where the outside hind leg swings forwards in readiness for the next canter stride.

(See Figure 1.7)

Figure 1.7 *Heinrich and I in a good balanced canter in right lead. The left hind started the sequence and the diagonal pair of the right hind and left fore come to the ground just prior to the right leading fore.*

Collected canter

In collected canter the canter steps are short and the horse appears uphill in his carriage, with the poll the highest point. This canter makes the horse easy to manoeuvre, especially with advanced movements such as canter pirouettes.

Working canter

Working canter is the horse's 'normal' canter, i.e. the one in which he can feel confident and relaxed and should be able to work on the bit. A good working canter must be established before introducing any degree of collection or extension.

Medium canter

In medium canter the horse lengthens his stride, bounding forwards with energy (impulsion) while maintaining balance and rhythm.

Extended canter

An extended canter is a bolder version of a medium canter, and the horse should be allowed to lengthen his frame and to stretch his neck and nose forwards so that he can cover as much ground as possible.

Collection and extension are covered in detail in Collection, page 174, but are mentioned briefly below in exercise 3.

Tracking up

What is tracking up?
Tracking up is where the hind feet step into the hoof prints left by the front feet.

In collection, a horse will not track up because the steps will be short but active; for example, a horse in piaffe will not track up as the hind feet are taking a lot of weight and therefore the steps are quite short.

- In working gaits, and in medium walk, a horse will, or should, track up.

- In extended gaits, the horse may overtrack when the hind feet step over the prints of the front feet.
- On a circle, in working gaits, the horse's inside hind should track up. The outside hind will not, as it has to work on a larger circle than the inside hind.
- On straight lines, both hind feet should track up equally.

(See Figures 1.8 and 1.9)

Factors affecting tracking up

Tracking up can be an indication of the correctness of the horse's gaits and how he is working through his back, but it is very important to take into account how the whole horse is working and not just looking at where he places his feet. Conformation can also affect whether the horse tracks up or not. A horse with a long back and short legs will never be able to track up, though he may be working correctly through his back and into the bridle. On the other hand, a horse with a short back and long legs will always track up or even overtrack even if he is not working correctly; hence the importance of assessing the horse as a whole and not just looking at where he is placing his feet.

Figure 1.8 (right top) *Tracking up on a straight line when both the hind feet step into the prints of the forefeet.*

Figure 1.9 (right bottom) *This horse is not quite tracking up: the hind foot does not reach the print of the forefoot. He has dropped his poll, is slightly behind the bit and is a little on his forehand, despite his uphill conformation. This could easily be rectified with a few half-halts to put more weight on his haunches, which will lighten the forehand and raise the poll.*

Tempo

> **What is tempo?**
> Tempo is the speed of rhythm.

One of the best ways to experiment with tempo is to ride to music. Select tracks that you like that have different tempos, i.e. with a fast beat or a slow one and try walking, trotting and cantering to fast and slow music. The rhythm should be regular, but you will need to slow down or speed up to fit with the music. This is changing the tempo. The rhythm must not alter. Practise this on the flat as well as over ground poles, cavalletti and small jumps.

Loss of energy, or impulsion, affects the quality of the gaits. The steps become laboured, and lacking in spring or elasticity, though the horse may still work in a rhythm. Going too fast can affect the expression of the horse, with the steps becoming short and hurried, even though the rhythm may still be regular.

 # Exercises to Improve Rhythm and Tempo

Exercise 1 (dressage and jumping)
Lungeing
AIM
To assess and improve your horse's natural rhythm in all gaits using ground poles and cavalletti or raised poles. Using poles can be very beneficial when improving your horse's way of going. Equally placed poles can really help the horse remain in rhythm when working through various ground patterns.

Before commencing the exercises, loosen your horse on the lunge on a circle of about 15m. This can be done without any extra equipment or, if he is a bit fresh, a chambon can encourage him to use his top line and belly muscles and limit the amount he misbehaves. If he is correctly muscled you can use side reins to work him on the bit once he has settled. (See my book *The Problem-free Horse* – J.A. Allen – for further details on lungeing.)

It is your choice whether you do the following exercises with your horse stretching forwards and downwards or on the bit. Ideally he should be able to do both. Aim to start with stretching work, then work on the bit and finish with stretching work again.

THE EXERCISE
Set four cavalletti or ground poles parallel to each other at walk distance apart (0.8m [2ft 6in]) and then lay four ground poles in a star shape so that the horse can go over them on a large circle (about 15m). The inner ends of the poles should be 8m (26ft) apart. This gives you two different patterns to work with. (See Diagram 1)

Exercise 1a
Begin by walking your horse over the four parallel cavalletti or poles; cavalletti are particularly useful for this as they do not roll should the horse touch them and he will very quickly learn to pick up his feet and to flex his leg joints. This has the added benefit of increasing the horse's back movement and improving suppleness, which in turn helps him to relax and work in a rhythm.

Exercise 1b
After the horse has walked over the cavalletti in each direction, lunge

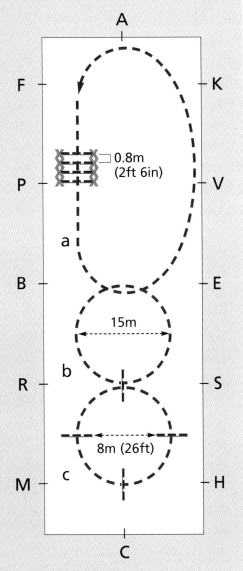

Diagram 1 *Exercise 1 Lungeing over poles or cavalletti.*

him on a circle over the ground pole of the star shape nearest the cavalletti in trot. Guide the horse towards the walk cavalletti again and ask for the downward transition to walk just before them. Repeat this on both reins.

Exercise 1c

Walk over the star shape on a circle. Initially, aim to place the horse so that he walks over the centre of each pole, so the circle is a true circle and not an oval! Then progress to decreasing and increasing the size of the circle which will in turn alter the number of steps the horse takes between the poles.

Repeat this exercise in trot and canter. Return to walking over the cavalletti frequently to give the horse a break from just working on a circle and to introduce transitions.

WHAT TO LOOK FOR

A horse working in a good rhythm should appear to cover the ground smoothly and without any alteration in rhythm or length of stride. The horse's steps will be more pronounced over the poles but the rhythm should remain the same whether going over the poles or not.

TRAINING TIPS

- Make sure your horse stretches properly forwards and downwards. A correctly muscled horse should do this easily. If your horse is incorrectly muscled (see page 19) then he may either come behind the vertical, or hollow his back. In either case, pole work on the lunge will help him improve his outline and balance.
- If you are using side reins, make sure your horse is working correctly on the bit with his nose vertical or just in front of the vertical. He should look exactly as he does when he is ridden under saddle, if you are doing it properly, of course!
- Make sure your lungeing circle is level when you are making a basic assessment of the gaits. Sloping ground can affect the horse's rhythm, but can be used as a more advanced form of training at a later stage, and is especially useful for jumping training for the event horse.

- Give your horse a chance to settle down and work off any excessive freshness first and give him a chance to settle into his stride.
- Work for sufficient time to allow the horse to understand what is required of him and to use his body and mind constructively. He should be tired, but not exhausted. His heart and breathing rates should increase during the work phase, and return to normal during the stretching phase. This will get the horse fitter, and the rider; with all the running around lungeing takes more effort than you think and is not the easy option!

PROBLEM SOLVING

- If your horse has an uneven stride or takes irregular steps, he may be tense. Make frequent transitions to help him to relax generally and to relax through his back. This should improve his rhythm. If the problem persists, or he is actually lame, consult your vet.
- Your horse may have a better rhythm on one rein than the other. To help with this issue, make frequent changes of direction, and try altering the size of the circle from large (15m or even 20m) to small (10m), and back to large.
- You may find that your horse bends his neck too much in one direction and looks to the outside in the other. His rhythm will be affected, and he will look as though he is falling in or drifting out. This is a sign of stiffness (or natural crookedness – see Straightness, page 147) and is rectified by using even-length side reins. Having the inside side rein shorter to encourage bending usually just gives the horse something to lean on and he will tend to fall in.

(See Figure 1.10)

Figure 1.10 *Lungeing your horse over poles is a very good way of assessing his natural rhythm. Once he has loosened up and settled into his work, he should then work calmly, in each gait, taking even steps; this is his 'natural' rhythm. Here Norman is showing active steps over a pole on the ground. Pole work helps to develop cadence and rhythm.*

Exercise 2 (dressage and jumping)
Schooling with ground poles
AIM

To develop and improve your sense of rhythm and to remain in harmony with your horse at walk, trot and canter.

THE EXERCISE

Lay out a sequence of ground poles or cavalletti as shown in Diagram 2. If you have enough poles and/or cavalletti, do a separate layout for each gait so that you can switch between them in a single training session. Alternatively, you could use a different one each day if you prefer. Place the walk poles in a corner and the trot and canter poles so you can use each section individually or string them together in a sequence. Lay out the walk poles in a fan shape so that the middles of the poles are 0.8m (2ft 6in) apart. The trot poles are 1.3m (4ft) apart, and the canter poles 3.5m (11ft 6in) apart. (See Diagram 2 and Figure 1.11)

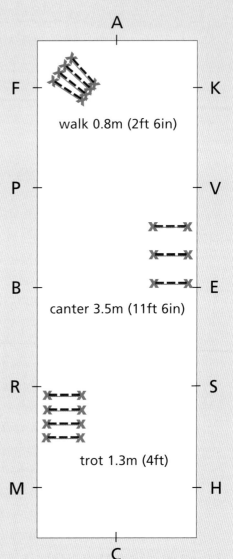

Diagram 2 *Exercise 2 Schooling over ground poles in each gait. Pole/cavalletti layouts and distances for walk, trot and canter. Place the walk poles in a fan shape in a corner and the trot and canter poles so that you can use each section individually or string them together in a sequence. Lay out the walk poles in a fan shape so that the middles of the poles are 0.8m (2ft 6in) apart. The trot poles are 1.3m (4ft) apart, and the canter poles 3.5m (11ft 6in) apart.*

Figure 1.11 *Once your horse is happy with ground poles, you could introduce cavalletti into his training regime. If your horse is not used to cavalletti, lunge him over them for a few training sessions so that he is accustomed to them before you attempt to ride over them. Cavalletti really help to develop a horse's strength through his back and flexibility of the joints, both of which are necessary for him to work in a rhythm. Here Norman gives cavalletti work his best shot, working with impulsion in a correct outline in side reins.*

Many horses attempt to jog over walk poles at first, especially if they have not become used to them when being lunged. Placing the poles in a fan shape in the corner of the school will deter the horse from jogging because he is approaching the poles on a curve and not heading off into open space.

Go over the trot poles in either a light (forward) seat or rising trot to start with. Once your horse is strong in his back, then you can do them in sitting trot. Mind you, you must have a good seat yourself so that you do not disturb the horse's rhythm and balance!

For the canter poles, a light seat is best. Maintain a steady contact with the bit, just enough for the horse to work in a rounded novice outline, i.e. accepting the bit with his nose just in front of the vertical. Sit upright coming in on the approach, and afterwards to maintain the pushing power from behind (*Schubkraft*)

WHAT TO LOOK FOR

The horse should take even, regular steps of the same length and quality over each pole. Ride over them in a balanced, controlled manner in each gait, making sure you keep your horse straight and working into a steady contact.

TRAINING TIPS
- Aim to maintain the horse's walk, trot and canter before, during and after the poles. You should feel some improvement in the horse's

balance and confidence after going over poles, and he should be more active within his natural rhythm.

- Practise riding in a light or forward seat. This can be invaluable in allowing your horse to work though his back so that he remains in rhythm. If you are out of balance, you will affect his rhythm.
- Make sure the poles are spaced at distances suitable for your horse's gaits. Wrongly placed poles can cause confusion. The distances between the poles are: walk 0.8m (2ft 6in) apart; trot 1.3m (4ft) apart; canter 3.5m (11ft 6in) apart.
- Start with single poles spaced around the school. If the horse has a good rhythm, the step over each pole will not be obvious. If he hops over them, this can be a sign of tension or stiffness. Pole work will help to rectify this problem, and improve the horse's suppleness, thus improving the rhythm.
- Placing poles in a fan shape works well for trot and canter poles as well as walk poles and increases the engagement of the inside hind leg.

(See Figure 1.12)

PROBLEM SOLVING

If your horse panics when faced with a sequence of ground poles, space them at twice the distance apart, i.e. canter distance 3.5m (11ft 6in), which allows for a step between each pole. If the horse breaks into canter, the poles will still 'fit' his stride, so he will be less likely to panic.

If your horse tends to hollow his back over the poles then you need to spend some time working on his outline and ability to work through his

Figure 1.12 *Working over ground poles is just as valuable for dressage as jumping. Set three or four poles consecutively at the correct walk, trot and canter distances (see text). You can build up to eight poles if you have enough! Practise riding over the poles, maintaining the rhythm, without speeding up or running out of energy.*

back (see Suppleness, page 61). Working in a correct outline over poles, and also stretching him forwards and downwards, will help to improve his rhythm.

Exercise 3 (dressage)
Altering tempo
AIM
The aim of this exercise is to explain the difference between altering tempo (the speed of the rhythm) and transitions within the gait (not altering the speed of the rhythm, but the type of walk, trot or canter). Changes of tempo within the gait should be at the same rhythm, e.g. you could have a slow, normal, or fast collected walk.

'**Changing gear**' from one walk to another or one trot to another (**altering the length and height of stride**) while **maintaining the same tempo and rhythm** is a very useful exercise. Remember that what a stride loses in length it must gain in height (see Impulsion, page 117). Instead of one gear of, in this example, collected or working trot, go up through the gears as in the following examples. This applies to all types of walk, trot and canter.

Example one – changing the **type of trot but not the speed**.
First gear: **collected trot** → Second gear: **working trot** → Third gear: **medium trot** → Fourth gear: **extended trot**

Example two – different gears creating subtle **changes within the collected trot**, which helps to improve the quality of the collected trot and helps the rider to find the horse's 'best' or optimum collected trot.
First gear: **small** collected trot (extra engagement) → Second gear: **normal** collected trot → Third gear: **big** collected trot (more forwards). (See Figure 1.13a,b and c)

This exercise can apply to the walk and canter as well, and you can put in as many gears as you like. The aids you require are collecting and extending aids (see Collection, page 174).

To **change tempo**, use the gears exercise in a different way by **altering the speed of the gait but not the type**, as follows.

Example three – First gear: **slow** collected trot → Second gear: **normal** collected trot → Third gear: **fast** collected trot.

Example four – Fourth gear: **slow** working trot → Fifth gear: **normal** working trot → Sixth gear: **fast** working trot, and so on.
(See Figures 1.13a, b and c)

Again, this exercise can apply to walk and canter also. You need to maintain the aids for each gait, but slow down and speed up your hip movement accordingly, so that both you and the horse are doing the same speed. If you get out of sync with the horse and start pushing with your seat, or bouncing up and down, then the horse will become tense, which will affect the rhythm. If the horse is working though his back properly you should find it easy to sit in the saddle and if you are sitting well, then the horse will work through his back properly!

Figures 1.13a, b and c *Heinrich shows the difference between collected, working and medium trot steps. Riding the different types of trot around a corner can really help the engagement of the hind legs, as the inside hind has to take weight on the turn. Make sure you ride this exercise on both reins to work the hind legs evenly. a) (above left) Collected trot with a shorter, higher outline. b) (above centre) Working trot with a slightly bigger frame. c) (above right) Medium trot with a bigger outline still; the frame lengthens as does the stride.*

THE EXERCISE

Exercise 3a

Changes within the gait on circles; these exercises can be ridden in walk, trot and canter. From the halfway marker on one side of the school (this is shown in the diagram on the long side, but you could do it on any side, or from the centre point at X) ride different-sized circles, each at a different gait. Start with a 15m circle in, for example, medium walk, then progress to a smaller one (10–12m) in collected walk. Go back to the 15m circle in medium walk and then make a 20m circle in extended walk. Try to make a clear transition into each walk at the same point where the circles start on the track. Repeat the exercise in trot and then in canter. (See Diagram 3a)

Exercise 3b

Ride a 10m circle in a corner in collected walk, trot or canter. Then proceed across the diagonal line in either medium or extended walk, trot or canter. Repeat on the other rein. (See Diagram 3b)

WHAT TO LOOK FOR

Changing tempo does not mean going from collected trot, to working, then medium. You can have a slow or a fast collected trot without it becoming a working trot, for example. You have to bear in mind the qualities of a collected trot; there must be: an uphill appearance to the horse's outline, clear engagement from the hind legs, and shortened, springy steps (see Collection, page 174). These qualities should remain while you ride either faster or slower.

TRAINING TIPS

- Make sure you develop your horse's ability to take weight behind with half-halts and transitions before you attempt this exercise (see Contact, page 86). This will help him to slow down and speed up without falling on his forehand and becoming unbalanced (see Figure 1.14).
- To increase the difficulty of this exercise, change tempo every three strides, i.e. going faster or slower in each gait, this speeds up your

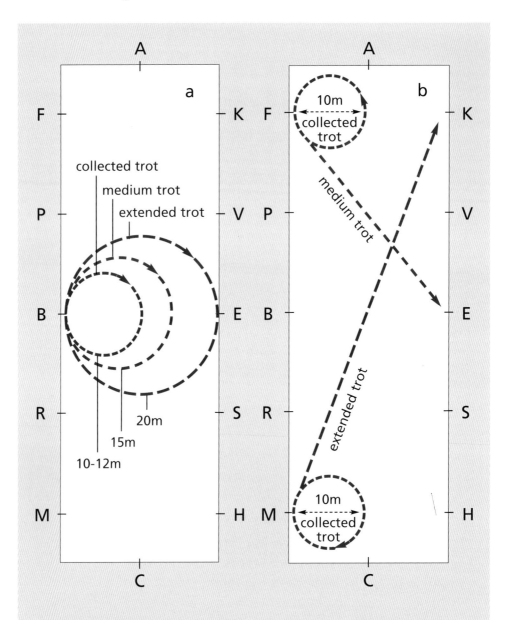

Diagram 3 *Exercise 3 a) Changes within the gait on circles. b) Changes within the gait from circles to straight lines.*

reactions and improves your ability to give the aids effectively and quickly; all of which helps to preserve and improve the sense of rhythm.

● In trot, alternate between rising trot and sitting trot every few steps. If you aim for every three steps, you will find that you will have to

Figure 1.14 *Taking weight behind is an essential element to changing tempo. Amadeus and I demonstrate how a horse looks when he takes weight behind. Note the uphill appearance of the whole horse, especially his back as his haunches lower and flex, so that the forehand is clearly raised. The poll is the highest point and his*  *nose exactly on the vertical. I am supporting him with my position and rein contact without restricting the horse's movement or willingness to go forwards. My position is upright and I am sitting exactly in the middle of the horse's back. If a horse is taking weight behind correctly, he will go forwards willingly without needing to be driven forwards with the rider sitting back as is so often seen.*

maintain your leg position and aids throughout, i.e. keeping your legs on whether you are rising or sitting. It is all too easy to forget to maintain the leg aids when you are sitting. Also, make sure you keep your rein contact consistent. This exercise is harder than it sounds and it really fine-tunes your aids and position!

- In canter, ride three steps in the saddle, and three steps in a light seat. It is easier to ride six steps of each, but if you aim for three, it does not give you time to become complacent. It is all too easy to wait for the 'right moment' to find that you have gone around the whole arena without doing anything. If you wait forever you will never improve! Increasing your ability to switch from a light seat to sitting will help you to feel when your horse needs your seat to assist him to use his back more effectively underneath you. A light seat helps him to stay relaxed. The end result should be a horse who can work through his back in a relaxed way: the prerequisite of maintaining rhythm! (See Figure 1.15)

Figure 1.15 *Riding in a light seat frees your horse's back thus helping him to remain relaxed during his work. It is a useful seat for work over poles and cavalletti. A good way to introduce a rider's seat to a young horse is to alternate frequently between sitting in the saddle and riding in a light seat with the seat just out of the saddle. This horse's nose could be more forward.*

PROBLEM SOLVING

- If your horse runs when you ask him to speed up, practise riding more slowly in each gait first to improve his balance and make sure he is working into a steady contact and using his back properly. (See Suppleness, page 61)
- If your horse finds it difficult to change tempo while maintaining rhythm make sure you are using your hips properly (see pages 24–25). You have to ride with the horse and do the same walk, trot or canter with your hips that the horse is doing with his hind legs. The horse cannot do extended trot if your hips are stiff and cannot move with him. You will just end up bouncing around on his back, making him tight in his back, and so he will just run away with short steps and not extend through his shoulder.
- Loss of rhythm can be caused by tension, so try asking for just a few steps at a slower or faster tempo. For example, on the circles exercise, just ask for a quarter or half of each circle at a different tempo and then resume normal tempo rather than trying for a whole circle straight away (see the training tips above).

Exercise 4 (dressage)
Maintaining rhythm in lateral work
RIDING 'IN POSITION'

In order to ride lateral movements correctly, it is important to be able firstly to 'position' the horse (ride the horse 'in position'), i.e. position him with a correct bend through his body and flexion at the poll both to the right and to the left. This positioning, or working from the inside leg to the outside hand as it is commonly known, prepares your horse for any circle, turn, corner, transition, or lateral movement. Riding in position is the first degree of bend; shoulder-fore requires a little more bend and shoulder-in requires more bend through the horse's ribs. Positioning your horse straightens his natural crookedness.

Invisible aids are used to ask the horse to work into the outside aids from the rider's inside leg, so that the inside rein can be softened without dropping the contact. Despite the slight degree of bend, to the onlooker the horse appears straight. Once you can position your horse equally to the right and to the left, you will then also be able to ride him absolutely straight with the hind feet stepping into the tracks of the front feet, into an even contact.

When you change direction, you need to change position. When riding on straight lines, as well as circles, make sure that your inside leg is used at the girth (your toe should be level with the girth) to keep the horse working into your outside aids. If he *is* working into your outside aids, your inside rein will soften. Make sure you keep his ears (poll) level. Once he is in position, his inside leg will be stepping forwards under his body and taking weight, which is why the inside rein softens; his weight is transferred from the rein to his back leg. Positioning the horse on both reins, making frequent changes of direction, will ensure you end up with a supple, straight horse!

To ride your horse in position:

- Place your inside leg with your toe level with the girth and use it to support your horse, pushing his ribs *in the direction of your outside hand*. Thinking of this in these terms helps to keep the inside leg at the girth as it applies inward pressure and should not, therefore, swing back as is commonly seen. Your inside leg also keeps the horse going.
- Place your outside leg slightly further back (half a boot length) to prevent the haunches swinging out and to support the horse's ribcage on the outside. Thus the horse not only works into your outside hand, but also your outside leg.
- Keep a steady contact with your outside rein to support the horse's outside shoulder and to keep the neck in line with the body.

- Encourage the horse to chew by using a soft finger movement on the inside rein, and ask for a barely perceptible flexion to the inside at the poll so that you can just see the horse's inside eye. If your horse is properly flexed (positioned) in this way, you should be able to soften your inside rein without the horse losing balance, tipping his head or changing his outline with the poll as the highest point.
- Sit level on both seat bones to control both sides of the horse's back and both hind legs.

(See Figure 1.16)

Figure 1.16 *Heinrich is in inside position on the track with his inside hind leg stepping forwards under his body and slight flexion at the poll to the inside. He is kept in position by my position, i.e. inside leg at the girth, outside leg behind the girth, upper body slightly turned to the inside – note the inside rein is yielded slightly so Heinrich works in balance and correctly into my outside aids.*

Only a horse who is supple (loose) and straight (able to bend equally in both directions into an even contact) will be able to maintain his rhythm. A degree of collection is also required so that the horse remains balanced.

AIM

To ride a combination of lateral movements in patterns around the arena, maintaining rhythm throughout in each different gait.

THE EXERCISE

The following exercise can be ridden in walk, trot or canter and on both reins. A change of lead in canter will be required each time the exercise is performed on a different rein.

Ride shoulder-in on the long side for a few steps. Proceed in half-pass to the centre line. Ride shoulder-in down the centre line for a few steps. Proceed in half-pass to the track. Once you are on the track, proceed in shoulder-out for a few steps before straightening the horse and repositioning him to the new inside-bend shoulder-in. (See Diagram 4 and Figures 1.17a, b and c)

SHOULDER-IN

The shoulder-in develops collection in a horse, teaching him to take more weight on his haunches.

The shoulders are brought to one side, the right or the left, of the haunches so that the horse is travelling forwards and sideways. When viewed from the front, three legs can be seen, i.e. the horse is on three tracks with the inside hind and outside foreleg on the same track. This angle is maintained by your position, i.e. your upper body (hips and shoulders) are angled to the right or left, bringing the horse's shoulders in, i.e. in off the track, or line of travel.

To ride a shoulder-in to the left, horse and rider are positioned to the left as though to do a small circle. To ride a shoulder-in to the right, horse and rider are positioned to the right as though to do a small circle.

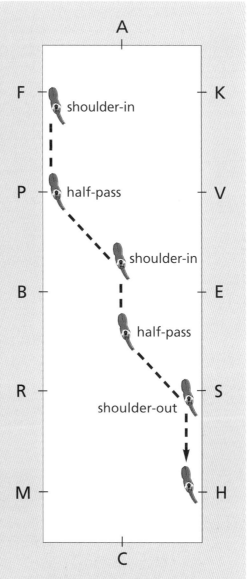

Diagram 4 *Exercise 4 Maintaining rhythm in lateral work: shoulder-in to half-pass.*

Figure 1.17a, b and c *Heinrich demonstrates the exercise, starting in shoulder-in, proceeding in half-pass to the other side of the school, performing a few steps of shoulder-out, then changing bend into shoulder-in at the track after the half-pass. Note how the bend of the horse remains the same in the first two photos, and the second shoulder-in is a mirror image of the first. A supple horse like Heinrich should be able to bend equally in both directions. a) (above left) Ride shoulder-in on the long side for a few steps. b) (above centre) Proceed in half-pass across the school. c) (above right) Change the bend into shoulder-in at the track after the half-pass and shoulder-out.*

Aids for shoulder-in

Position your horse, establishing correct bend and flexion (see page 46). Use the inside leg at the girth to ask the horse to step forwards and sideways into the outside rein. This creates bend in the horse's body through the ribs, resulting in the inside hind leg stepping forwards under his belly. Your outside leg behind the girth keeps the horse's body angled off the track and your outside rein contact prevents the horse actually turning onto a circle.

The rider's body angle maintains the angle of the movement. Your hips and upper body are turned as one unit to the inside (of the bend of the horse) to bring the horse's shoulders to the inside of the track of his haunches so that his outside front leg is on the same track as his inside hind leg (hence 'shoulder-in').

Your hands should remain parallel maintaining a steady contact. The only thing that your reins do is to ensure that the horse's head and neck are in line with his body bending away from the line he is travelling along. The horse steps sideways away from your inside leg; the outside rein will feel slightly firmer as the horse bends around your inside leg; and the inside rein will feel a little softer as the horse takes more weight on his inside hind, transferring weight from the rein contact to his haunches. If the horse is correctly balanced, you should be able to give a little on your inside rein without the horse changing his outline or rhythm. (See Figure 1.18)

Figure 1.18 *Amadeus in shoulder-in. We are both correctly positioned with our shoulders to the inside, but I could have a bit more weight in my inside stirrup and could be sitting taller with my ribs lifted. Note that Amadeus is working on three tracks with his inside hind leg and outside foreleg on the same line or track.*

HALF-PASS

To ride half-pass from shoulder-in, position your horse (see pages 46 and 47) and then increase pressure with your outside leg to push the horse's haunches into your inside aids. The horse steps sideways towards your inside leg; your hands should remain parallel maintaining a steady contact; the inside rein will feel a bit firmer as it supports the horse and the outside rein needs to be softer to allow the horse to go in the direction in which he is looking. The horse's forehead should be on the line he is travelling along.

To summarise: shoulder-in is ridden inside leg to outside hand, and half-pass is ridden outside leg to inside hand, with the horse in the same position or bend.

WHAT TO LOOK FOR

The horse should remain in the same rhythm throughout the exercise and stay in position the whole way through the exercise. There should be no change of flexion or bend until the horse completes a few steps of shoulder-out at the track at the end of the second half-pass.

By maintaining the position throughout the exercise, the rider can ensure the correctness of the half-pass and the shoulder-in/shoulder-out and the regularity of the rhythm. The horse should also remain in balance. Any loss of balance, i.e. falling on the forehand, will affect the rhythm.

TRAINING TIPS

Positioning your horse ensures that he becomes accustomed to working properly into your outside aids. This positioning prepares your horse for any circle, turn, corner, transition, straight line or lateral movement. When you change direction, you need to change position.

To ride your horse in position:
- Place your inside leg with your toe level with the girth and use the inside leg to support your horse and to keep him going.
- Place your outside leg a few inches further back to prevent the haunches swinging out.
- Keep a steady contact with your outside rein to support the horse's outside shoulder and to keep the neck in line with the body.
- Ask for flexion to the inside with a soft finger movement on the inside rein – just enough for you to be able to see the horse's inside eye. If your horse is properly flexed in this way, you should be able to soften your inside rein without the horse falling in. If he falls in, use more inside leg and outside rein.
- Keep your weight evenly on both seat bones to control both sides of the horse's back and both hind legs. Sitting too much on your inside seat bone can make the horse unbalanced.

(See Straightness, page 147)

- When riding this exercise, try to be as accurate as possible; make sure each shoulder-in is on a straight line on three tracks, and each half-pass is on a diagonal line with the same bend as the shoulder-in. (The more advanced the horse is in his half-pass, the 'straighter' he is, i.e. with his body parallel to the long side. A less experienced horse will need to lead with his forehand somewhat in order for him to remain relaxed and rhythmical.) This ensures that the lateral movements have the same degree of difficulty, making it easier to maintain the rhythm. If the angle is too steep for the horse, then he may well lose rhythm.
- When ridden in canter, this exercise can be a very good suppling (loosening) exercise in preparation for changes of leg through trot or walk or a flying change. Make the transition or the change as you reach the track at the end of the shoulder-out, making sure you straighten the horse properly beforehand. After the change of lead, reposition the horse to the new inside bend. (**Note** A horse should be straight when performing a flying change to ensure he changes cleanly. If you concentrate too much on changing the bend, then the horse may lose balance and the rhythm of the canter will be lost.)

PROBLEM SOLVING

- If the horse is ridden with too much neck bend in his lateral work, he will not be correctly bent through his ribs around your inside leg, which will affect his balance because he will tend to fall onto the outside shoulder in any lateral movement. The way to correct this is to make sure the horse is ridden in position properly, as described earlier.
- If the haunches swing away to the outside, then you must prevent this happening by using sufficient outside leg behind the girth.
- If the horse speeds up or slows down, changing tempo, then you need to make sure you are regulating the tempo with half-halts and maintaining the walk, trot or canter movement with your hips. Horses often speed up if you become tight in the hips, or alternatively too heavy in the saddle, collapsing through the torso.

Exercise 5 (jumping)
Jumping on a circle
AIM

The aim of this exercise is to develop rhythm over evenly placed jumps on circles of different sizes. This exercise works very well with ground poles, cavalletti or small jumps. When jumping on a circle, the horse should maintain a consistent bend and balance in order to reach each jump correctly for take-off. Because the jumps come in quick succession, you have to concentrate on placing the horse for the next obstacle quickly and efficiently. The jumps are equally spaced around each circle, allowing the same number of non-jumping strides between each, thus helping horse and rider to maintain rhythm.

It is important that you establish a rhythmic, balanced canter with a degree of collection so that the horse can take his weight behind.

Try the exercise in trot before proceeding to canter. Working in trot can give horse and rider confidence and enables you to plan the route around the circle, aiming the horse at the middle of each jump.

THE APPROACH/TAKE-OFF/LANDING

For a horse to make a good jump over an obstacle, it is most important to give him the best chance possible. Your aim should be to get him to the jump straight, in a good rhythm, and with enough weight on his hocks to propel himself into the air. If you look down at the base of the jump, so will he and he may well stop. Try to anticipate him doing this; if you feel him hesitate, give a firm leg aid, followed by a quick tap with the whip if necessary, and if you have one. Alternatively you could ride with spurs to reinforce your leg aids. Stay cool and calm, and approach the consecutive jumps as though nothing happened. If you have a problem, try to wipe it from your memory, and start afresh with the next approach.

In the air, remain quietly in balance. Fold from the hips so that your upper body is low with your stomach over the horse's withers. The higher the obstacle, the lower your upper body should be. Make sure you move your hands forwards to allow the horse to stretch his neck forwards as he jumps.

As the horse lands and puts his forefeet on the ground, close your knees and calves against the saddle and brace your thighs. Your joints act as shock absorbers, and cushion your upper body. Stay low with your upper body until you feel the horse's back legs touch the ground. The momentum of his hindquarters coming underneath him will bring your upper body upright again. If you are tight in your hips, however, this will not happen and you will pitch forward. Keep your weight evenly distributed in your stirrups to balance yourself and the horse.

If you come upright too soon, before the hind legs have touched the ground, your horse will land short and too much on his forehand, his neck will rise too early, and his hind legs will drop and knock the top rail of the jump.

If you lean to one side, you will not be in a good position to approach the next jump. Bring your hands back to the normal position by the withers and keep the horse into the bridle with your legs. Ride away from the jump to make a fresh approach to the next one. Avoid leaning on the horse's neck with your hands. This spoils your rein contact and can result in the horse hollowing his back, raising his neck, and falling on his shoulders on landing. This may seem insignificant over a pole, but it will put him very much on his forehand over a big jump. Your weight will be too far forward and you may well end up banging your nose on his neck!

When riding a series of obstacles on a circle, you have to be able to react quickly between landing and taking off again. If you remain in a forward seat all the time, you will find that you get more forward over each jump, and end up falling forwards over the horse's neck. As you land over the first jump, bring your upper body back up and keep your seat in the saddle. You will then keep the horse on his hocks ready for the next take-off. Remember to rebalance the canter with a half-halt on the non-jumping stride or strides.

THE EXERCISE
Lay out small jumps or cavalletti as shown in Diagram 5. (To start with, poles on the ground may be useful for establishing rhythm.) Raise two

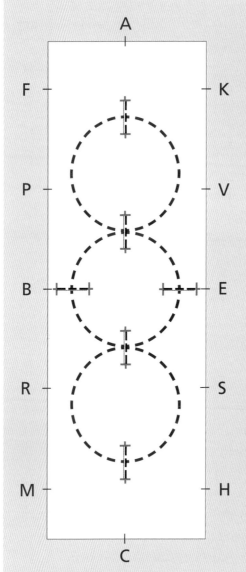

Diagram 5 *Exercise 5 Jumping on circles to establish rhythm. The circles should be 15–20m in diameter.*

jumps at a time, until all six jumps are raised. They do not all need to be the same height. The final height depends on the capability of horse and rider, but an ideal height for training purposes would be 0.8m (2ft 6in).

WHAT TO LOOK FOR

The small jumps divide the circle into four. You should be trying to achieve a well-shaped circle (i.e. round!) with each quarter of the circle the same shape as the preceding one. You should aim to take the same number of strides in each quarter of the circle and, if all the strides are the same length, this gives you the rhythm. It is a very good way to learn how to jump in a rhythm, which is essential for any show-jumping course.

TRAINING TIPS

● Get the canter right; try not to go too fast or the canter strides will become flat and the horse will be on his forehand. To help maintain balance, alternate between trot and canter when riding the circles over the jumps. If the canter is too slow and lacking in energy, then your horse may not have sufficient impulsion to make it over all four jumps without breaking gait. You should be able to go around the circle over the jumps three times in a row before needing to stop. Conversely, you do not need to go around it over and over again too many times. If you and your horse get too tired, you will make mistakes.

- Make sure you alternate jumping on circles with other work round the school to ensure your horse uses different muscles. Also, change the rein frequently and allow your horse to stretch at regular intervals.
- Start with ground poles or low jumps to get the rhythm, balance, and line of approach on the circle to ascertain that you have set them out evenly around the circle and your horse can take each one in his stride.
- Miss alternate jumps out if you or your horse is finding it too difficult, or jump one obstacle, go around the next on a small circle, and then jump the next, and so on. The circle around the jump can be in trot or walk if you wish. This is especially useful for keeping the horse calm and responsive to your aids.
- Make sure you work on both reins so that you develop your horse's muscles evenly on both sides of his body.

PROBLEM SOLVING

- If your horse is knocking the jumps, it is commonly a result of going too fast, which puts the horse on his forehand. Take some time to improve the canter with transitions to trot and walk before returning to the exercise again. Aim to ride three or four times around the circle over the jumps before having a break and doing something else.
- If you are finding it difficult to turn around the circle, try riding around outside the jumps a few times to establish bend, and make sure your horse is working in position, before resuming the exercise. If your outside aids are not supporting the horse, then you will have difficulty in keeping him straight. (See Straightness, page 147)
- If you are losing impulsion (see Impulsion, page 117) take a break from the exercise, and work around the arena changing canter within the gait: collected canter for four strides, working canter for four strides, medium canter for four strides, and so on. This can also be ridden in trot and walk in between the jumping exercise to give the horse a break.

Exercise 6 (jumping)
Cavalletti or small jumps
AIM

The aim of this exercise is to maintain rhythm on each rein over a sequence of jumps on a straight line.

THE EXERCISE

Cantering over cavalletti, or small jumps, is a great way to establish and maintain rhythm and tempo.

Lay the grid out as shown in Diagram 6. Start the grid with three cavalletti or trot poles set at 1.3m (4ft) apart. These help to bring the horse calmly into the grid in trot to eliminate the risk of him rushing. Lay the first of four cavalletti or small jumps at 2.5m (8ft) from the last trot pole. This will bring the

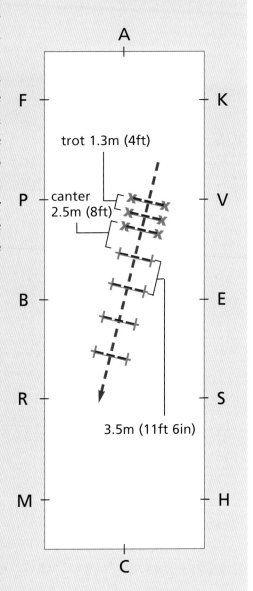

Diagram 6 *Exercise 6 Gridwork (gymnastic jumping). Cantering over cavalletti, or small jumps, is a great way to establish and maintain rhythm and tempo. Place three trot poles or cavalletti set at 1.3m (4ft) apart. Lay the first of four small jumps at 2.5m (8ft) from the last trot pole or cavalletti. This will bring the horse in at the right stride for the first small jump. Set each consecutive small jump at 3.5m (11ft 6in) apart, which gives you a series of small bounce jumps without a non-jumping stride in between. The jumps should be no more than 90cm (3ft) high. Ride in a light, forward seat so that you do not disturb the horse's balance. The jump comes in the period of suspension of the canter.*

Figures 1.19a–d *Cantering over cavalletti; a great way of developing rhythm and tempo. Rachel Waine and her Connemara pony Storm tackle a row of cavalletti. Her light seat position is very good: her lower leg remains in the same position throughout, and she allows with her hands at the right moments so as not to disturb Storm's rhythm and balance.*

horse in at the right stride for the first small jump. Set each consecutive small jump at 3.5m (11ft 6in) apart, which gives you a series of small bounce jumps without a non-jumping stride in between. This is extremely effective gymnastic work for any discipline! (See Diagram 6 and Figures 1.19a–d)

WHAT TO LOOK FOR
Your horse should take even, regular steps, taking the poles and cavalletti in his stride. He should accept the contact and jump with a rounded back, with his neck reaching forwards to the bit. He should remain calm before and after the grid. Approach the grid in trot and then allow the horse to

break into canter over the cavalletti. He should do this of his own volition as long as you keep your legs on! Look ahead into the distance. Aim your line of sight over the last cavalletti onto the line you will be following afterwards. After the grid, bring the horse quietly back to trot and walk, preferably on a straight line to keep him balanced. Then turn away back up the school for another attempt. Aim for three or four successful times over the grid and then resume other school work before trying three or four times again. Always finish an exercise on a good note before the horse is too tired to perform well. There is always another day!

TRAINING TIPS

- Make sure the poles and cavalletti are set out at the correct distances for the horse. He will then remain relaxed and be able to maintain his rhythm.
- As a rider, you should ensure that you are able to maintain a light, balanced seat throughout the exercise so that you do not disturb the horse's balance. As there are no non-jumping strides in this exercise you can remain in a light seat throughout the grid.
- You should be flexible enough in your leg joints to absorb the movements of the horse's back as he bascules (rounds his back) over each obstacle.

PROBLEM-SOLVING

- If your horse struggles with the distance, then increase or decrease the distance between the cavalletti accordingly.
- Should he panic or become unbalanced when you start to introduce canter work then spend longer working over ground poles in trot at his natural rhythm and tempo.

2 Suppleness (Looseness – *Losgelassenheit*)

Suppleness is the most common translation of the German word *Losgelassenheit*. A better definition would be 'looseness of mind and body'. Looseness gives the impression of fluidity and 'freeness' in the movement of the horse. This can only happen if the horse is mentally relaxed and confident enough to let himself go. It is most common to find Rhythm placed first in the scales of training, but some schools of thought, particularly in the older training regimes of horsemanship, are that *Losgelassenheit* should be established before the horse can work in a rhythm. This does seem logical; only a loose horse can work in a rhythm. A tense horse is likely to lose rhythm and take uneven strides and not work through his back. He will most certainly not be 'mentally loose' or relaxed.

This quote is taken from Waldemar Seunig's book *Horsemanship* published in 1956 (J.A. Allen): 'A horse that is psychologically and bodily cramped will find it hard to flex and relax its muscles elastically…'

From a psychological point of view, in order for a horse to show *Losgelassenheit* he must first of all trust his rider, otherwise he will not be able to relax and let himself be trained in the state of *Durchlässigkeit* or 'throughness'. This aspect of training is commonly called submission or obedience to the rider's aids and is often misunderstood. If a horse is *forced* to submit to the rider, then the scales of training go out of the window. Riding has to be a partnership between horse and rider, not the rider dominating the horse, as is all too often witnessed. Of course, there has to be discipline, but on the part of the rider as well as that of the horse.

Tension has to be understood in the right way. There is good, or necessary, physical tension, which is essential for muscle function, and bad tension which is basically a state of mind, i.e. anxiety. Relaxation should be a mental state rather than physical. The mind should be relaxed in order for the body to work to its full potential. The muscles have to contract (tense) and extend (relax or stretch) in order to create posture and movement. Without any tension at all, the horse's muscles would collapse in a heap like an unset jelly and not be able to support the skeleton. A horse who is expressing himself and showing pizazz is not tense in a detrimental sense, and should not be penalised for showing off providing his gaits, outline and way of going are correct and he is basically enjoying himself, i.e. he is mentally relaxed!

Only the rider who adheres to proper training guidelines, i.e. the scales of training, will gain the respect and trust of a horse. The horse needs to learn to react to the rider's aids in order to perform to the best of his ability, and he can only do this if he understands the rider's requests. Horses are not born disobedient, but they can switch off as a form of mental self-defence and react adversely if they find an exercise physically too demanding. The rider then has to go back a stage in the training, to re-affirm easier exercises before progressing again. The horse will let you know what the problem is; all you have to do is to understand the horse! You will know when you have achieved the balance between discipline and reward as the horse will relax in his work, trust you and be willing to oblige. In other words he is loose, relaxed and 'through', i.e. showing both *Losgelassenheit* and *Durchlässigkeit*.

For the horse to be truly loose, it is important that the rider has a good understanding of how the horse moves and how he carries the rider. Otherwise, how can the rider fully comprehend the intricacies of a good seat and how the aids influence the horse?

From a physical aspect, suppleness (looseness) is the flexibility of the horse, particularly of his spinal column. This can be put into two categories: lateral (side to side) and ventral (up and down) (see Figures 2.1, 2.2 and 2.3). The spine is not uniformly supple along its length. Starting at the poll, the atlas joint allows the nodding action of the horse's head, and the axis joint allows side flexion: the ability to rotate the head from side to side.

The neck is the most flexible part of the spine and can bend right around to the side of the body. This is how your horse can scratch his hind leg with his teeth. Restriction of the neck movement affects the looseness of the horse as a whole. If the neck muscles are not loose a horse cannot relax and stretch forwards (see Figure 2.4). The horse must be allowed to use his neck as a balancing pole, even in collection. The neck shortens

Figure 2.1 *Lateral suppleness on a circle. Amadeus showing his ability to bend from nose to tail on the line of a circle. Both Amadeus and I are correctly positioned for the circle but I could be sitting a little taller and looking between the his ears!*

Figure 2.2 (right top) *Ventral suppleness. Amadeus tucking his pelvis and bending his hind leg joints as he takes weight behind in preparation for piaffe. He is uphill through his body, and his neck and head are in a correct outline with his nose just on the vertical and his neck raised and arched forwards and upwards with a light forehand. I could sit up straighter though, and keep my foot in my inside stirrup!*

Figure 2.3 (right centre) *Norman showing suppleness through his spine from his nose to tail. His belly muscles are toned and he is tracking up and moving freely through his shoulders: a good example of a 'loose' horse.*

Figure 2.4 (right bottom) *A horse should be able to relax forward to the rein offered. Jo is asking Trevor to start to stretch and the muscle definition on Trevor's neck, and the rest of his body, is obvious.*

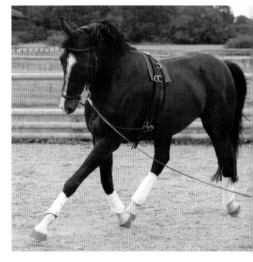

and arches to correspond with the horse tucking his pelvis or 'sitting' as he takes weight behind. The length of rein has to allow this arching of the neck, not create it by pulling the head in. (This leads on to contact; see Contact, page 86)

The withers are inflexible. The thoracic spine, to which the ribs attach, is most flexible where the rider applies the leg aids. Behind the saddle, the loins are flexible at the thoracic-lumbar joint. The next flexible part is the lumbo-sacral joint where the spine connects to the pelvis.

It is important to allow a horse to stretch forwards and downwards frequently during training to relax the whole spine, maintaining flexibility and suppleness through the back in particular (see Figures 2.5a and c).

The flexibility of the leg joints plays a very important part in the looseness of the horse as a whole. The placement of the legs under the body is crucial to the horse remaining in balance on turns and circles as well as on straight lines. The leg joints must be able to bend in order for the horse's hind feet to follow the tracks of his forefeet. (This is also the key to straightness, demonstrating how the scales of training link together.)

A stiff horse will not be able to place his feet under his body and remain in 'four-wheel drive' at all times, i.e. he will become crooked (see Straightness, page 147).

The Effect of Stretching on Suppleness (Looseness)

We translate the German word *Losgelassenheit* as 'suppleness' and it should be translated as 'looseness'. In my opinion, therefore, the scale should be Looseness, not Suppleness. Suppleness is the result of working through the scales and should be translated as 'throughness' or 'working through the back', i.e. *Durchlässigkeit*.

Correct stretching is a true indicator of how loose and relaxed the horse actually is. In order for a horse to move well, his back muscles have to be relaxed, i.e. extended. If your horse can stretch forward and down with his neck fully extended when he is moving, then his back muscles are relaxed, allowing his dorsal spine to lift (see Figures 2.5a, b and c). A horse who is worked properly on the bit will voluntarily stretch his neck forwards and downwards. A horse who is worked behind the bit or above the bit will not be able to stretch properly.

The horse's spine is supported from underneath by the abdominal muscles. As his spine lifts, his loins coil under, and his hind legs come under his haunches. His hind leg joints become more able to flex and carry weight. By extending his neck and supporting his forehand with the muscles surrounding his withers the horse is able to move freely through his shoulders and relax through his poll, jaw and mouth. This ability to stretch through the back is the foundation of training your horse to work into the bridle and for creating a horse with true *Losgelassenheit*.

  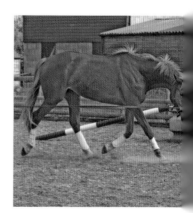

Figures 2.5a, b and c *a) (above left) Trevor stretching forwards and downwards correctly when ridden with the nose forwards, which lifts the horse's back. The belly muscles are taut and the loins lifted. b) (above centre) Trevor showing a natural stretch forwards and downwards when grazing in the field. c) (above right) Archie stretching on the lunge. His belly muscles are taut, his back raised, his nose forwards and downward with his hind legs under his body, showing lovely freedom of movement through the shoulder and good relaxation.*

The biggest muscle in the horse's back is the longissimus dorsi. It is made up of many smaller muscles, giving it a huge range of movement enabling the spine to move up and down (ventrally) and from side to side (laterally). It has a right and left side so that each side of the horse's back can move independently, for example when each hind leg moves in turn. The spine is supported along its whole length by a system of ligaments, the main one being the nuchal ligament. I am not going into the anatomy of the back here – there are many good books on the subject – but you need to be aware of how the horse's back is constructed and how it moves! Ligaments are for support, muscles are for movement.

If you run your hand across the back muscles of a correctly trained horse, you should be able to feel the edge of this slab of muscle, rather like a saddle blanket of muscle. A horse with a violently bouncing back is often mistaken for one with a supple, swinging back, but in fact this demonstrates that he has weak loin muscles. In this instance, the back muscles are not strong enough to control the movement of the back; you would feel the spine with your hand, and the back muscles would feel soft rather than firm. Contracted back muscles on the other hand feel tight and hard as rock, which you would feel on a tense horse with a hollow back. The hind legs of the tense horse would be out behind in the paddling-duck position. The tail is a good indicator to tension in the back: the tail bones are the last section of the spine and so if a horse is working with a relaxed swinging tail you can bet that the rest of his back is working as it should be.

Jumping the horse, both under saddle and free, is invaluable for improving looseness whatever discipline the horse is used for. Watching your horse jump freely without the rider on his back can be a revelation if you have never seen him in action! A once-a-week free-jumping session should be part of every horse's training regime. The jumps do not have to be high, but should be big enough to make the horse really stretch through his back. Observe how the horse's neck telescopes forwards as the shoulders lift off the ground! (See Figures 2.6a–i)

The Rider's Influence on Suppleness (Looseness)

The mental state of the rider has a huge effect on the *Losgelassenheit* of the horse. A horse can only achieve *Losgelassenheit* if the rider is also in this state of relaxation, both mentally and physically. The rider should be calm and confident

Figures 2.6a–i *Jo and Trevor showing how valuable grid work is in improving flexibility of the horse's spine and the rider's ability to go with the horse. Note that Jo's lower leg position remains secure throughout, and she manages to fold with her hips over the fences. She allows her hands to follow the movement of Trevor's neck fairly consistently. She has come upright with her body a bit soon in photo (b) but has wisely given Trevor a looser rein so he can remain in balance. She recovers in photo (c) and balances him well between the fences. In photo (d) Jo maintains a supportive contact while allowing Trevor to arch his neck forwards. In photos (e) and (f) they are both in good balance on landing, enabling Trevor to maintain impulsion between the fences (g). She drops the contact slightly on the take-off (h), but makes a lovely jump over (i). Look at the sequence of photos again, this time looking at Trevor's spine and how he tucks his loins on both take-off and landing, and how he powers forwards in between the jumps.*

with sufficient muscle tone to maintain a good position in the saddle and apply effective aids. A relaxed rider does not mean a floppy rider! They should be mentally relaxed but physically they should be supple and well toned. The rider's muscles should be able to contract and extend to produce movement in the same way as the horse's muscles. Tight, tense muscles cannot do this, and the flow of movement will be impaired. A tense, stressed rider will not be able to produce a loose, relaxed horse. Putting such a rider on any horse, even one that has been correctly loosened by a skilled rider, will produce tension and destroy any trust and confidence that the horse had previously. Conversely, a good rider should be able to instil a sense of calm over a stressed, tense horse and be able to improve his state of relaxation to the point that he regains *Losgelassenheit*.

A rider must be able to synchronize their hip movements to the oscillations of both sides of the horse's back (see Rhythm, page 21 and Figure 2.7). It is also very important to maintain a quiet, steady contact with the bit, and to earn a horse's trust enough that he willingly works to the bit whether stretching down, or in a rounded outline (see Contact, page 86). This emphasises how important it is that the first three scales of training go hand in hand with each other: Rhythm, Suppleness and Contact.

Figure 2.7 *Norman and I show how the rider's seat must be able to synchronize with the movement of the horse's back in order to maintain balance. Working on a long rein, my seat is secure and I am supple enough through the back and hips to keep Norman relaxed and swinging through his back in his work.*

 ## Exercises to Improve Suppleness (Looseness)

Exercise 1 (dressage and jumping)
Serpentines

A serpentine is a series of loops joined together by a short straight line, or they can be curvy, i.e. from one bend to the other.

In a conventional serpentine, the loops that you ride should be even curves, i.e. part of a circle. These loops are joined together by a short straight line, which occurs as you cross the centre line each time. These few steps give you a chance to straighten the horse after each turn, and prepare him for the next. This has to be done smoothly so as not to unbalance him. Maintain the bend through the horse's body as you ride each loop, then half-halt, position yourself and the horse for the next turn, and then ride forward into the turn in a good rhythm.

In a curvy serpentine, loops join together with just one straight step. The loops can be ridden as large as you wish. The advantage of this serpentine is that it gives the horse the chance to really bend through his ribs on each loop, and the change of bend is more demanding. It is a great way to discover if your horse bends more easily in one direction than the other!

AIM
The aim of riding serpentines is to make frequent changes of bend between and over poles to improve lateral suppleness.

THE EXERCISE
Place four poles equally spaced down the centre line of the school, leaving sufficient space between them so you can ride through the gaps. The loops can be ridden in walk, trot, or canter. With canter, try to make a change of lead as you pass between the poles. This can either be a change through trot or walk (simple change) or a flying change. Be as accurate as you can with the change of direction. Aim to pass exactly between the poles each time. (See Diagram 7a and b)

WHAT TO LOOK FOR
Make sure that all the loops are the same size so that your horse has to bend the same amount in each direction.

TRAINING TIPS
● The loops on a serpentine, regardless of the number of loops, should be ridden as part of a circle. Make sure you position the horse correctly in the new flexion and bend (see Rhythm, page 21) before changing

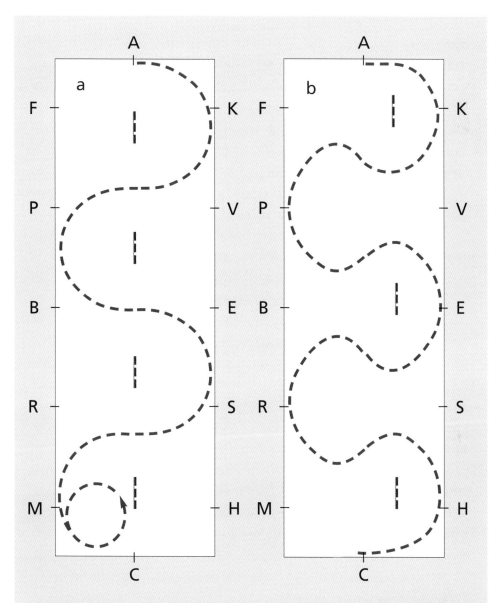

Diagram 7 *Exercise 1 Serpentines can be ridden between markers such as poles, and circles can be added in the loops to help lateral suppleness. a) Conventional serpentine. b) Curvy serpentine.*

direction and be ready to use the new inside leg and outside rein to help the horse balance (see Figure 2.8). Sloppy loops will not help the horse to track up (follow the prints of his front feet with his hind feet) and your loops will end up different shapes.

Figure 2.8 *Inside position when the horse is flexed slightly to the inside at the poll (lateral flexion) in preparation for a turn or circle. This is in itself a valuable exercise to improve suppleness.*

- A variation on the serpentine is to ride shallow loops between the poles, rather like riding a slalom. Turn around the end poles so that you can slalom your way up and down the poles two or three times. This really loosens the horse!
- A more advanced exercise is to ride serpentines without changing bend. This means that on the first loop you will be bending the horse to the inside, and on the next loop he will be bending to the outside. This takes some concentration on the rider's part, but it is an extremely good exercise for improving looseness. This version can be ridden in walk, trot and canter, but to do it in canter you need to understand how to maintain counter-canter.
- Counter-canter is deliberately cantering on the leading leg opposite to the direction of movement while performing certain school movements. It is a test of the horse's balance, strength and obedience to your aids. Prepare the horse for counter-canter by firstly riding frequent transitions into and out of canter, through trot first of all, then through walk. A forward-thinking collected canter is ideal for riding counter-canter. The horse must have developed some ability to keep his weight on his hocks in order for you to ride counter-canter. A useful preparation exercise to be done in walk and trot is shoulder-out. This helps you to feel the amount of bend the horse needs through his body. The shoulder-out position requires exactly the same angle as a good counter-canter.

PROBLEM SOLVING
- Make sure you position your horse properly at each change of direction. There should be at least one straight step when you can half-

halt to ensure that your horse is balanced. This straight step is also necessary for a good flying change.

- Inaccurate aids cause the loops to vary in shape, with the horse commonly cutting in on the first half (not enough inside leg) and bulging out on the second half (not enough outside leg). It is important to use both legs when riding serpentines to control both sides of the horse's ribs.

- Using too much inside rein can cause excessive neck bend and you will find that the horse drifts outwards on the loops. However, if the outside rein is used too strongly, then the horse will not be able to bend his neck at all. The happy medium is simply to maintain an even contact on both sides of the bit. The inside rein will soften slightly if the horse is working properly from behind and taking weight on his inside hind leg, thus alleviating the need to support the horse with the inside rein.

Exercise 2 (dressage and jumping)
Lungeing or riding over poles
AIM

To improve suppleness (looseness) through the back (ventral suppleness).

THE EXERCISE

Place four ground poles or cavalletti in a fan shape at one end of the school, i.e. the inside ends of the poles are closer together than the outer ends, with the middles of the poles 1.3m (4ft) apart. The horse should be able to trot over the poles at this distance. Moving the horse towards the narrow end will shorten his stride, and towards the outer end will lengthen his stride. This is a very good way to improve suppleness through his back. At the other end of the school, set out four poles or cavalletti parallel to each other, again at 1.3m (4ft) apart for trot work. (See Diagram 8).

The horse can either be lunged without any extra attachments or with a chambon or side reins. The chambon will encourage stretching, and the side reins will help him to work in a rounded outline.

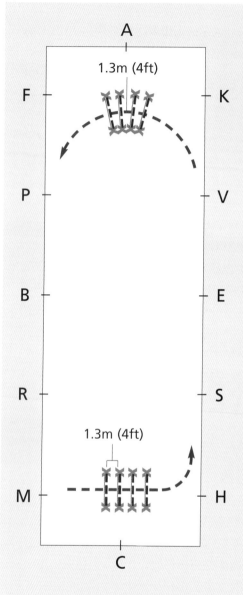

Diagram 8 *Exercise 2 Ground poles and cavalletti placed at opposite ends of the school to improve suppleness (looseness) through the back. The poles should be set out at the trot distance of 1.3m (4ft) apart.*

WHAT TO LOOK FOR

Start by loosening your horse with some lunge work for about ten minutes, with no extra equipment, and without going over the poles. Treat the two pole layouts as two separate entities. Most horses will find the parallel poles easier than the fan to start with, as only ventral suppleness is needed and both hind legs will be working the same amount. Do make sure that you bring the horse in to the poles as straight as possible and move with him so that you do not inadvertently drag him to the inside. The fan requires both ventral and lateral suppleness because the horse is stepping over the poles on a curve, which requires more engagement, or taking of weight behind, particularly on the inside hind leg. Alternate between both sets of poles, going over the poles 6–8 times in each direction. The whole training session should last 30–40 minutes (including two short rests) depending on how fit the horse is.

It is a good idea to spend half the session doing stretching work, and the other half working on the bit in side reins. Give the horse a break from the poles by either working him in canter or walk for a few minutes; this will ensure that the horse has a good work out and uses all his muscles as he should. Finish by letting him relax and stretch in walk.

TRAINING TIPS

- Lungeing in a chambon prevents the horse from contracting his back muscles and leaving his hind legs trailing, encouraging him to relax and stretch his neck correctly. A horse cannot hollow his back with his neck stretched. Circle work on the lunge requires lateral bending of the horse's spine, which he cannot do with a tight, hollow back.
- Make sure the side reins are long enough to allow the horse to work comfortably on the bit. If they are too short, they will restrict his ability to use his neck to balance and you may well find he knocks the poles.
- Make use of the school to give the horse frequent breaks away from the poles in order to give him a chance to use his new-found looseness in a relaxed manner and ensure that he gains confidence through the exercise.

PROBLEM-SOLVING

- If a horse is new to pole work, reduce the number of poles to one or three. If you are using two poles he might jump them; to deter him from doing this, double-space them to ensure that he takes a step in between them. Double-spacing with a line of poles (maximum of three) is also useful if the horse is likely to panic when faced with a line of poles.
- If the horse becomes tense when using side reins, you could try using just the outside one and attaching the lunge line directly to the bit, so that you are actively using the inside side rein. It is important that you keep a contact with the bit to prevent the horse from looking to the outside.
- If the horse tends to rush away, or even spin at you on the lunge, you could work him on the double lunge (long reins) for this exercise,

using your rein contact to keep him straight, and using half-halts and transitions to good effect between the pole exercises to keep him focused on the job in hand.

Exercise 3 (dressage)
Lateral work: shoulder-in and renvers/travers

You need to practise riding your horse in position (inside leg to outside rein) on straight lines and circles so that he works properly into your outside rein. This is essential before you ride any movement. (See Rhythm, page 21)

One of the key things to remember when riding movements is that the rider's inside aids are those on the inside of the horse's bend; the rider's outside aids are those on the outside of the bend of the horse.

SHOULDER-IN
(See Rhythm, page 21 for how to ride shoulder-in)

RENVERS (HAUNCHES-OUT)/TRAVERS (HAUNCHES-IN)

Renvers and travers (and half-pass for that matter) are basically the same movement, but the name changes depending on where in the school the movement is ridden. In both movements, the horse is positioned, or bent, so that he is looking where he is going. (In shoulder-in and leg-yield, the horse is facing away from the direction in which he is travelling.) If the horse's haunches are pushed away from the wall, then the movement is travers; if the haunches are pushed towards the wall, then it is renvers. The haunches are moved to either the right or left of the forehand so that they step sideways in the direction the horse is bent around the rider's inside leg, like a banana.

Aids for travers/renvers

Position the horse so that his forehand is approaching the wall with his head facing up the track. Your asking leg is your outside leg behind the girth, indicating to the horse to step along the track keeping his haunches in from the track. Your inside rein maintains the inside position. This is your dominant rein aid. Your inside leg maintains the bend in the horse's ribs, and asks him to keep going. The outside rein needs to soften to allow the horse to travel along the track.

To ride a renvers/travers to the left, horse and rider are positioned to the left as though to do a small circle. To ride a renvers/travers to the right, horse and rider are positioned to the right as though to do a small circle. (See Figures 2.9 and 2.10) See page 107 for a fuller description of the aids for travers.

Changing the bend
AIM
The aim of this exercise, using shoulder-in and renvers, is to change the bend through the horse's ribs from one movement to the next, maintaining the angle to the wall to improve suppleness and bend through the ribs. I call this my 'goldfish' exercise.

THE EXERCISE
On the left rein, after the short side, ride shoulder-in left from the corner for a third of the long side. Then change position to the right, and ride renvers for the

Figure 2.9 (right top) *The correct bend for renvers. This horse has his haunches towards the wall of the school. He is bent around the rider's inside leg and she is asking him to go sideways with her outside leg, i.e. the outside leg for the bend of the horse, and maintaining flexion at the poll with her inside rein. The renvers can also be ridden on a smaller angle with the horse on three tracks.*

Figure 2.10 (right bottom) *Travers is a mirror image of renvers. The haunches are positioned away from the fence, but the aids are the same as for renvers. Again, the angle could be decreased so that the horse is on three tracks. As with the previous photo, this is a good example of correct flexion at the poll.*

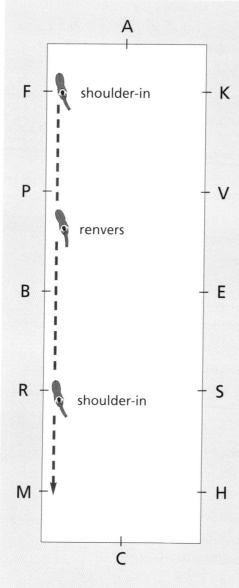

A

F — shoulder-in — K

P — — V

renvers

B — — E

R — shoulder-in — S

M — — H

C

Diagram 9 *Exercise 3 Lateral work: shoulder-in to renvers to shoulder-in; maintaining the angle but changing the bend.*

next third of the long side, maintaining the same angle of the horse's shoulders away from the wall. For the last third of the long side, change position again to the left back to shoulder-in. Repeat on the other rein using shoulder-in right, and renvers left. (See Diagram 9)

WHAT TO LOOK FOR

Make sure you change the emphasis from 'inside leg to outside rein' for shoulder-in to 'outside leg to inside rein' for renvers. Also make sure you switch your leg position, which will transfer your weight to your new inside stirrup, as you change from one movement to the other. Remain sitting equally on both seat bones.

TRAINING TIPS

- Use the corner to position your horse correctly for the first shoulder-in. If necessary, put in a small volte of 8–10m to set the horse up.
- This exercise works well in walk and trot. Make sure you keep the horse balanced with half-halts, especially as you change position from one movement to the other.
- You could also ride this exercise up the centre line, making sure you

maintain angle and position. This is more difficult as you do not have the support of the wall, but it is a very good test of your position and aids.

PROBLEM SOLVING

- Many problems with lateral work arise because the rider's body position aids are not accurate enough. A lot of riders are tempted to use too much inside rein, pulling the horse's neck to one side and riding 'neck in' rather than shoulder-in. This just causes the horse to fall out through his outside shoulder and then the rider needs to use a huge amount of outside rein and leg to correct the horse. It is far easier for the rider to position the horse with their upper body, particularly the hips, in the first place. Without controlling the outside of the horse properly, the bend in the ribs will be lost, and the value of using lateral work to improve suppleness will be lost.

- The rider should be aware of sitting on both seat bones in lateral work. Many instructors emphasise that the rider's weight should be on the inside seat bone. In my experience, this causes many riders to lean in and lose control over the outside hind leg. It can be helpful to concentrate on sitting on both seat bones in order to control both hind legs. The rider's weight transfers slightly to the inside *stirrup* if the rider turns their hips correctly.

- The rider's outside leg should be a hand's breadth behind the inside leg. The inside leg should be positioned so that the rider's toe is level with the girth. The rider's outside leg should be placed further back *from the hip,* not by bending the knee and bringing just the lower leg further back. Instigating the movement from the hip has the effect of turning the rider's hips into the correct 'inside position'. The rider's inside leg at the girth has two functions: it gives the horse something to bend around, and also asks the horse to keep going.

Exercise 4 (dressage)
Changes of rein through the circle
AIM

The aim of this exercise is to improve suppleness and dexterity by changing the position (bend) of the horse within the confines of a circle. As you change direction, make sure you ride one straight step on the centre line. This ensures the horse is straight and balanced before you change position (bend).

THE EXERCISE

This exercise is divided into two sections. Firstly, ride a 20m circle at one end of the school. Then change the rein through the circle, changing position as you reach the centre of the circle, and ride the circle on the other rein. Aim to ride the full circle two or three times before changing the rein.

The second part of the exercise is to ride a small figure-of-eight. This involves changing the rein at the centre of the figure where the two circles touch. This exercise can be ridden in walk, trot and canter. Of course when riding this in canter, you have to ride a change of leg either through trot or walk (simple change) or with a flying change. (See Diagram 10)

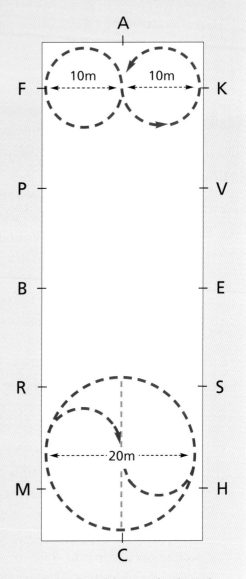

Diagram 10 *Exercise 4 Changes of rein through the circle and figures-of-eight. Ride one straight step on the centre line as you change direction.*

WHAT TO LOOK FOR

- The change of rein through the circle should be made by riding two small half-circles, or demi-voltes, within the larger circle, rather like the pattern on a tennis ball. The exact moment the bend of the horse is changed should be at the centre point of the circle. The first demi-volte should commence at one of the quarter points on the circle, and the second demi-volte should finish at the opposite point on the other side of the circle, dividing the bigger circle into two.

TRAINING TIPS

- Make sure you ride accurate circles to start with, maintaining the correct positioning of the horse. As the horse becomes looser, then the size of the larger circle can be reduced to 15m.
- The demi-voltes should join together with just one stride on a straight line to allow the rider to half-halt and to reposition the horse.
- The figure-of-eight is a progression from the change of rein through the circle. Just think of repeating the change of rein each time you reach the centre point.

(See Figures 2.11a and b)

PROBLEM SOLVING

- If your horse is not loose enough to cope with changing the rein within a circle, then start by changing the rein out of the circle. Ride a half 20m circle to the centre point of the school, change position, and then ride a half 20m circle in the other direction. This can then be expanded into a large figure-of-eight.

Figures 2.11a and b
Accurate circles are essential to developing suppleness. a) (above) Preparing to ride a small circle. Both horse and rider are facing in the direction of travel. Use of the outside aids will ensure the horse brings his shoulders around the circle. b) (right) Correct bending on a circle. Note that the horse's nose is exactly in line with the middle of his chest and both horse and rider are looking around the circle line.

Once you can do this in each gait, try the exercises again. Always start a new exercise in walk, as this gives you the time to make sure the horse is bending properly (correct positioning).

- Make sure your horse is relaxed throughout his work. Remember, a tense horse is not a loose horse.
- Make sure you maintain the rhythm of the gait. The horse should not alter rhythm and tempo throughout the exercise. Correct his balance with half-halts (see Contact, page 96) to help you to maintain balance as you change from circle to circle.

Exercise 5 (jumping)
Changes of direction over single jumps
AIM

The aim of this exercise is to improve the horse's (and the rider's) ability to turn sharply, remaining in balance through the changes of direction. The smaller the turn the more the horse must be able to bend in his ribs and to take weight on his haunches (see Collection, page 174). It is not so much the height of the jumps that is important but the technique with which they are ridden.

The rider's position is very important (see Rhythm, page 21). It is vital that the rider can remain in balance with the horse at all times. Jump training does not always go to plan: if the horse does make a mistake, the rider must be able to help the horse by maintaining their position and by being able to switch from a light, or forwards, seat to sitting upright in the saddle in a split second so that they can use the back and hip aids as necessary. It is very important to keep a secure lower-leg position, so that the appropriate leg aids can be applied when needed.

THE EXERCISE

The exercise is split into two parts. Firstly, set two jumps opposite each other so they can be jumped on a 20m circle from both directions. Jumps such as an upright and a parallel that look the same from both sides would be very useful. The height of the jump depends very much on the level of training the horse has reached, but I would suggest a minimum height of 0.5m (1ft 6in) and a maximum of 1m (3ft). The parallel can be from 0.5m (1ft 6in) up to 1m

(3ft) wide. The exercise can be ridden in trot or canter. A change of rein through the circle can be ridden between the jumps and can involve a transition to help the horse to keep his weight behind (collection) which helps to lighten the forehand and make it easier for him to turn: for example, trot–walk–trot or canter–walk–canter, or a flying change.

The second part of the exercise is to place three jumps as shown in the diagram at right angles to each other, so that they can all be jumped in sequence as a mini course. The change of rein occurs over the middle jump. You can incorporate both sections of the exercise together which will test your ability to change direction in quick succession and improve the horse's lateral suppleness. (See Diagram 11)

WHAT TO LOOK FOR

Ride the exercises in trot to start with. This gives you a chance to get your line to each obstacle absolutely correct. Aim to place the horse at the middle of each fence. Try to make sure that the horse is straight one stride before and after each one; this ensures that he can take off with equal thrust from both hind feet, and land safely on both front feet taking the same amount of weight on each leg. When the horse is in canter the front legs will land one

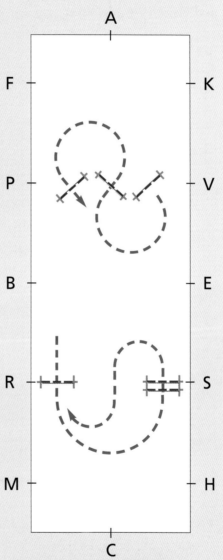

Diagram 11 *Exercise 5 Changes of direction over jumps. The two jumps on the circle can also be jumped a few times in the same direction to establish consistency of bend (position) in the horse.*

after the other, remember. Try to establish a bouncy, collected canter that is easy to control, and gives the horse the best chance of jumping well. If the canter is easy for you both, then you will be relaxed. Do not forget that *Losgelassenheit* applies to your state of mind at all times!

TRAINING TIPS

- The line that you ride on the ground between each fence is either going to be part of a circle or a straight line. If necessary, walk the course before you ride it so you can choose the most appropriate line of approach to each fence.
- The two jumps on the circle can also be jumped a few times in the same direction to establish consistency of bend (position) in the horse. Make sure he is working correctly from your inside leg into your outside hand.
- Make the changes of direction as neat and accurate as possible. Make sure you change direction with at least one straight stride so that you can change your horse from one bend (position) to the other easily. This avoids you 'flipping' him from one direction to the other. Turning your horse too sharply in training can have further repercussions in competition: for example, turning too suddenly on slippery going which may cause him to slip or even fall.

PROBLEM SOLVING

- If either you or your horse becomes tense, take a break from the exercise and stretch your horse in walk on a long rein. Try to avoid getting into this situation by jumping each exercise three times in a row, then doing something else around the school, riding in and out of the jumps, for example, at a different gait.
- If your horse gets too exuberant, try doing your canter work around the jumps until he is settled and then jumping from trot. Once he is calm, you can jump from canter again.
- If the horse is not forward going, take some time to work on transitions in quick succession to 'spark him up'. Chasing him round and round in canter will not help but just make him tired, causing him to switch off even more.

Exercise 6 (jumping)
Gymnastic grid work
AIM

Grid work, or gymnastic jumping, is invaluable, whichever discipline the horse is destined for, and should be part of every horse's basic training. Grid work improves flexibility through the back – ventral suppleness – and teaches the horse how to bascule over fences.

THE EXERCISE

Lay a gymnastic grid as shown in the diagram. Set four trot poles or cavalletti at 1.3m (4ft) apart at the beginning of the grid. Then place a cavalletti 2.5m (8ft) away from the last trot pole, and follow this with a further three cavalletti or small jumps at 3.5m (11ft 6in) apart, giving a total of four bounce jumps with no non-jumping strides. After the last bounce fence, put an ascending spread 7m (23ft) away, followed by another small ascending spread, 0.8m (2ft 6in) wide and 0.8m (2ft 6in) high at the back rail at the same distance, 7m (23ft). Approach the grid in trot, and let the horse break into canter at the first bounce jump. Maintain the canter through the rest of the row of gymnastic jumps. (See Diagram 12)

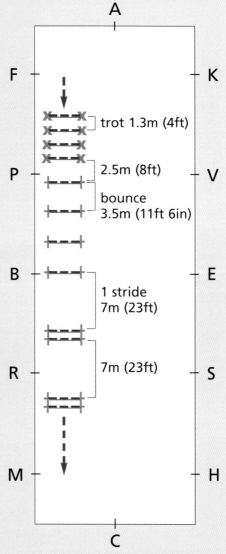

Diagram 12 *Exercise 6 Grid work with trot poles/cavalletti, bounce jumps and spread fences.*

WHAT TO LOOK FOR

You need to make sure you come into the beginning of the grid with enough impulsion to get you over all the jumps. This does not mean coming in fast, but your horse needs to have enough strength and power to thrust off his hocks. You need to work on getting your horse to take weight behind and to tuck his pelvis so that he is used to working with his hind legs under his body. As a rider, you must be able to maintain your jumping seat, and be able to fold neatly and quickly at the hips to go with the bascule of the horse. Remember to sit up on non-jumping strides so that you can half-halt the horse and make sure he remains in balance, not on his forehand, through the grid.

TRAINING TIPS

- If you jump the grid on one rein in one training session, build the jumps so they can be jumped in the other direction the next time you do grid work. This ensures the horse is trained equally on both reins.
- When setting out the grid, place all the poles on the ground to start with so that you can have a dummy run at the grid in trot and canter to check the distances before you raise the jumps and to familiarise the horse with the exercise.
- If your horse is new to grid work, add one fence at a time. You may not achieve the whole gymnastic row the first couple of times, but you should be able to build up to it over a few sessions.

PROBLEM SOLVING

- Jumping a sequence of jumps in a grid requires straightness from both horse and rider. If the rider leans to one side, the horse will jump to one side.
- Ascending spreads are inviting fences for the horse. If, however, the horse is rather bold and 'attacks' the ascending spreads, replace them with two small parallels, which should make the horse more careful and bascule better in the air.
- The approach and get-away from a grid must be straight. Approaching

a line of fences too fast and on a curve is asking for trouble, and your horse will most likely run out halfway down. This will ruin his confidence, make him tense, and you will lose *Losgelassenheit*. Calmness, relaxation, and accuracy are so important. To ensure the horse uses his back well, he must take off from both hind feet at the same moment.

3 Contact (*Anlehnung*)

Contact is not solely about focusing on the horse's mouth and holding the reins. *Anlehnung* is the German equivalent of Contact in the scales. Its literal translation is 'support'. This sums up the whole concept of contact in one word. (See Figure 3.1)

The rider has a contact with the horse through the hands, seat and legs, all of which are essential to maintaining the horse's balance and allowing him to work into a supporting rein. Many riders try to force the horse's neck into a round outline without any regard for the rest of the horse, and do not seem to care that the hind legs are paddling along behind. The horse should work into the rein, not against it. This can only be achieved if the rider grasps the concept of asking the horse to work from behind and in self-carriage. For the horse to work forwards the contact must be correct. Many riders misconstrue 'forwards' as speed in miles per hour and concentrate on that, not considering the horse's balance. Reins that are loose and jiggle around are just as detrimental to the horse as are strong rein aids that 'hold' the horse in an outline. Both prevent the horse from going forwards to the bit, and neither scenarios offer a supportive contact: the former is inconsistent, and the latter is restrictive.

The rein contact should never be stronger than the seat and leg aids. The reins should never give an aid in isolation without the backup of seat and leg aids.

Figure 3.1 *Contact is not just about the reins; I ride Amadeus into a correct contact with the seat, legs and reins working in unison. My hands are neither pulling back nor dropping the contact, but simply maintaining a contact with the horse's mouth.*

The Horse's Outline

It is very important that a horse can work through his poll correctly; if he does not do so, he will not relax his jaw. At whatever level the horse is working, he should appear flexible where his skull joins his neck. If you have a look just behind your horse's ears you will see and feel two 'bumps'. (You can see this most easily from the saddle.) These bumps are the rear edge of the skull and form the poll (the occipital crest). As the horse flexes at the poll and brings his head into a vertical position these bumps should be the highest point of the horse's neck.

The atlas bone (first neck vertebra), from which the horse flexes (nods) his head up and down, is situated just behind and below the poll. The axis bone (second neck vertebra) enables the horse to flex his head from side to side. A false outline occurs when the horse is worked overbent when the poll is dropped and the horse bends his neck several inches behind the poll between the second and third vertebrae.

The nuchal ligament, which supports the spine along its length, starts at the poll and finishes at the base of the tail. This is why the tail carriage is so indicative of tension or relaxation in the horse. If a horse is working properly through his back and into a correct contact, the tail will be relaxed and swinging. If he is not working into a correct contact, the tail will be tense and either clamped down, held stiffly to one side, or raised up. It might seem a little odd to look at the tail to see if the horse is working into the contact, but this just bears out the point that the contact affects the whole horse!

The horse's mouth and the bit

Developing a correct contact with the horse's mouth requires 'feel' and this has to be learnt and developed according to the rider's stage of riding. Initially, a novice rider learns to hold the bit steady so that the horse has a still bit to take a contact with. This is in itself quite a tricky business and requires quite specific instruction from a knowledgeable trainer who is himself able to establish and maintain a steady contact. Once this is attained, the rider progresses to being able to 'hold and soften' at exactly the right moment for the horse to yield to the bit (chew the bit) and to accept the bit without resistance. The horse's lower jaw bone has two sharp ridges of bone which form the bars of the mouth where the bit lies. These are incredibly sharp, and covered by the gums. A bit in rough hands can really damage this area and pulling can easily cause bruising. Rough rein aids can make this area really sore and even split the gums.

Every horse is different, although the rules of establishing a contact in the right way are consistent. It is the degree of 'hold and soften' that varies, also the length of time one should 'hold' and the speed at which to release and soften. A sensitive horse will react to slight variations in rein and body contact, whereas a horse who is less sensitive to the aids will require firmer aids with clearer difference between them for him to take notice. Every horse can be fine-tuned to accept a light, elastic contact, but this is entirely dependent on the finesse of the rider. A ham-fisted rider will never produce a horse who is willing and happy to work into the contact on the bit. A skilled rider will however be able to create a silk purse out of a sow's ear. The only way this cannot be achieved is if the horse has a physical or mental issue that is deep-seated and time has to be taken to erase bad memories.

The more complicated the bit, the better a rider must be. Whacky bits that bend this way and that and twizzle around only disguise a rider's bad hands. A rider that can maintain a steady contact with a simple snaffle is a rider who will progress to the double bridle at the appropriate stage of the horse's training, when more finesse is required in true collection. A good test is to ride in a straight bar snaffle with a cavesson noseband. The horse should go with a closed mouth without it being strapped shut with a tight noseband. Many riders are under the impression that strapping the mouth closed tightly disguises tension in the mouth. Unfortunately the whole horse will be affected by tension in the mouth because the back will tighten and the hindquarters disengage. It is common in this circumstance for the rider to drive the horse faster 'into the bridle'. Unfortunately this puts the horse *against* the bridle, causing resistance. Then comes a stronger bit, sharper spurs, and so on. The simple solution for the horse is for the rider to learn how to ride!

The horse's mouth should be taken into consideration when selecting the thickness of bit. For example, a horse with a fleshy tongue may go well in a thinner bit not because it is sharper – a bit is only as sharp as the rider's hand – but because it gives the tongue more room. It is possible to damage a horse's mouth with a plastic bit if it is used incorrectly. A skilled rider can use a double bridle with its bridoon and curb bits with sensitivity and the understanding of how the bits work together to produce a correct outline with the poll the highest point.

The level of training influences the outline

The horse's outline should change according to the level of training, but this does not mean compromising on the horse working properly at any level: he should be on the bit and working through his back, with his poll the highest point. The hind legs and forelegs should be synchronised, i.e. the horse should appear to be working the same with his hind legs as his forelegs, and not looking 'flashy' in front with the hind legs trailing behind.

A novice horse will be in a longer, lower outline than an advanced horse and should appear evenly curved through his top line from ears to tail. His neck should be in a lower carriage, but on no account should he be behind the bit. If he is overbent, he is not working properly from behind.

A horse's carriage at elementary level should appear slightly more uphill than a novice horse's carriage, and a medium horse's more uphill than that of an elementary horse, and so on up to advanced level. An advanced horse will appear much more uphill and shorter from nose to tail, because he is better able to take weight on his hocks and to collect.

In order for a horse to *become* more advanced, he must be able to take a great deal of weight on his haunches, which enables him to lift his forehand. Just lifting the neck position with the reins will do the horse no good at all and his back will become flat and tight.

Developing a horse's outline

It takes time to develop a horse's outline. A reasonable time scale is to aim to go up a level each year, i.e. one year at novice, the next at elementary and so on. During training it is important to remember to stretch your horse frequently with his nose forwards and down (not behind the vertical) to ensure the back muscles are being used properly. If the stretching work is not done correctly, your horse's outline, at whatever level you are working, will suffer as a result. No matter what level a horse is at in his training, he must be able and willing to stretch forwards and downwards to the bit on whatever length of rein the rider offers. If a horse is behind the vertical, he will not be using his back muscles properly and will never be truly working on the bit. He will also lose the ability to stretch his nose forwards and down, and will always tend to look at its knees – something a correctly trained horse will never do. (See Figure 3.2)

Figure 3.2 *Norman is stretching forwards and downwards into the contact and I am 'allowing the horse to chew the reins out of the hands' (aus der Hand kauen lassen). Note that he is still on a light contact at the very end of the reins – the horse should still be chewing the bit and not leaning on the reins. Norman is keeping his weight on his hind legs, working in balance with his nose reaching down towards the ground, and not looking back at his knees, which is often the case with many horses who are not trained properly. A correctly trained horse should always be able to stretch forwards and downwards like this. My heels could be lower!*

A lot of riders these days think that an overbent horse (who avoids the contact by tucking his chin in and dropping the poll) is on the bit. Nothing could be further from the truth. A horse who is neither allowed to use his neck properly nor allowed to stretch forwards and downwards frequently will develop both physical and mental problems. Such a horse will find it impossible to jump obstacles in a correct manner and may well suffer from back and neck problems as a result. A short tight rein will raise the horse's head and prevent him from basculing properly. The hind legs will trail and either get caught on a solid (cross-country) fence or knock a fence down in the show-jumping arena. The horse might find it very difficult to lift his shoulders and may well fall. On the other hand, not using the reins at all when a horse could do with a bit of support can be just as disastrous. A horse should be taught to accept the contact so that when a rider does need to give a rein aid, the horse responds as the rider wishes, and not by fighting the bit. To keep a horse properly in balance and on the rider's aids takes a lot of skill, especially when jumping, and co-ordination, and often a split-second reflex action on the rider's part is essential in tricky situations.

A correctly stretching horse will follow the bit as low as it is offered by the rider. (When a horse is under saddle this stretching is sometimes called 'working deep'.) This does not mean dropping the contact; it means lengthening the reins to the same length as the horse's stretched neck, with his nose reaching forward. His head should never be behind the vertical. If it is, then the poll muscles are under strain and the angle between the jaw and jowl is slammed shut, restricting space for the tongue. Bear in mind that a horse's tongue begins far back in his mouth and if he has no room to relax it, mouth problems such as teeth grinding or sticking the tongue out of the side of the mouth or over the bit are common. Strapping such a horse's mouth shut will only make the problem worse because once the tight noseband is off, the problems will worsen. The only remedy is to go back to stretching with the nose forward and down to the ground on the lunge so that the horse relaxes through his back and neck again. A quiet mouth is a sign of a correctly moving horse. Changing nosebands and bits in an effort to stop the mouth problem is futile if the problem lies in the mechanics of the horse's back movement.

 ## The Rider's Influence on Contact

The following applies just as much to the jumping rider as to the dressage rider; the rules are the same whether you are in the air or on the ground! If the rider's hands, arms and shoulders tighten against the rein contact with the horse's mouth, this will restrict the stepping under of the hind legs. For the jumping horse, a restrictive contact will diminish the pushing power of his hind legs on take-off, and affect the horse's bascule and height that he can jump. For the dressage horse, again the stepping under of the hind legs will be restricted, which will have a detrimental effect on the quality of transitions and also the ability to collect and extend the stride in any gait. Contact is the feeling of togetherness that the horse gives you not only through your hands but also your seat and legs, i.e. all the parts of you that are in contact with the horse.

Dropping the contact also has a detrimental effect on the horse's balance. If the horse is not supported by the rein when it is needed, i.e. the rider holding the bit quietly for the horse to reach towards, the horse will lose confidence in the contact and be reluctant to work into the reins, tending instead to back off the contact and not go forwards from the rider's leg and seat aids. Thus the horse needs the contact of seat, legs and reins in order to work with confidence under the rider.

The coordination of the seat, leg and rein aids

Many riders take up a contact without giving the horse a chance to loosen up through his back first. This can cause problems such as the horse overbending and coming behind the bit when the poll will no longer be the highest point, or the horse may shorten his neck and draw back from the bit, hollowing his back. In this case, the poll may be the highest point, but the withers will have dropped as the back tightens.

The amount and feel of contact is determined by the stage of the horse's education and his ability to work through his back and hindquarters. He should be working into the rein contact and not against it. A horse working incorrectly will be on his forehand and seeking support from the reins. This causes heaviness in your hands as he is trying to draw your weight over his front legs where his weight is as he is under the false impression that this is less effort for him. He is saying to you, the rider: 'please hold me up', but the message you want to give to him is: 'I will support you with my body, but not the reins alone'. To correct a heavy contact, counteract the rein pressure by closing your legs against the horse to keep them in position (from mid-thigh to mid-calf) and by bracing your lower back. In this way you can resist the horse's wish to drag you forwards and out of balance and use your body as the support mechanism that the horse needs. The aim is to remain sitting up tall with your stomach and back muscles toned and your elbows by your sides.

If the horse has drawn your arms in front of your body you will end up with aching shoulders as he uses you to support his forehand, and you risk getting into a pulling match, which you will undoubtedly lose! The amount of muscle tone in your whole body should be enough to prevent the horse spoiling your position. Sometimes this feels quite firm, especially if you are not used to using your core muscles to give you postural strength. If you have established this braced position effectively, the horse should react by taking weight on his hind legs. As he takes weight behind, his need to rely on the reins for support is diminished and so the contact lightens. (See Collection, page 174). Once the contact is lightened, you can reduce the amount of positional strength (muscle tone) in your body as it should be easier to remain in position. This bracing and softening is in effect a half-halt.

Let the horse show you the amount of contact he needs. If he is heavy on your reins increase your seat and leg aids to match. If he lightens the feeling on the reins correctly and chews the bit quietly then soften your aids. However, if he is avoiding the contact by tucking in his chin, thus making the bit rattle around in his mouth, take up the slack in the reins by shortening them initially and keep your legs on to encourage him to reach his neck forwards to the bridle so that he takes the contact and accepts the bit resting against his gums. Once the horse reaches forwards to accept the bit, his neck can be lengthened again by the rider offering the bit forwards and lengthening the reins slightly so that the horse is working with his neck as long as possible while remaining in a correct outline with the poll the highest point. (See Figures 3.3a–e)

When the horse accepts the contact and the length of rein you are offering him correctly, you must soften your aids in response to this acceptance. You do this by relaxing your arms so that your shoulder, elbow and wrist joints are flexible, enabling you to feel and work with the contact. This gives you the commonly termed 'elastic' feeling. If your arms jerk around or move forwards and backwards, the contact becomes inconsistent. If this happens, you no longer have a contact with the horse's mouth and he will have nothing to work into, thus his hind legs will trail, his back will hollow and he will no longer be working into the bridle or on the bit.

A light contact must come from the horse softening himself to you and not by him demanding that you give him the reins when he feels like it. The more balanced the horse, the lighter the reins become, even reaching the point where you can yield the reins completely from time to time to make sure that he remains in balance without relying on them at all. This is the test of self-carriage.

When riding school movements, preparing your horse for turns, circles and lateral work, it is important that you ride him in position from your inside leg to your outside hand (see Rhythm, page 21).

If the horse is working properly into your outside rein contact, you should be able to give a little on the inside rein to soften it but it should soften on its own if the horse is also stepping correctly forwards and under his body with his inside hind leg. The horse's weight is transferred from the inside rein to his inside hind, thus leaving the inside rein redundant. If the horse is leaning on the inside rein, he is not truly taking weight behind and you need to improve the horse's balance with half-halts. If the horse is truly balanced, you should be able to soften both reins without anything untoward happening. If the horse trips, rushes away or pulls at the reins, he is not on your aids. (See Figures 3.4a–e)

Figures 3.3a–e *These photos show both correct and incorrect head positions. a) This horse is above the bit and his back is hollow. This outline would improve with half-halts and transitions to help the horse lift his back and arch his neck forwards. The rider needs to keep a better contact with her legs to hold the horse up around the middle! b) The way to correct a horse with a hollow back is to encourage him to stretch forwards into a steady contact without shortening the neck at all. c) A demonstration of a horse behind the bit. d) This is the same horse as in (c) but here he is above the bit. e) The same horse again reaching forwards into the correct contact. His expression shows how much more released he is.*

Figures 3.4a–e *These five photos show how much the contact can affect how a horse works on a circle. a) Amadeus shows how a supportive outside rein, helps the horse to balance. The rider must also support the horse with the outside leg. b) A soft inside rein is the result of a horse working properly into the outside rein. This thoroughbred gelding is balanced enough to maintain self-carriage as the rider yields the inside rein. c) Dropping the outside rein gives Heinrich no support and so he will tend to lean on the inside rein and fall on his inside shoulder rather than take weight behind and work into the outside aids. d) Using too much inside rein causes Heinrich to tip his nose to the inside and he twists his head instead of flexing properly through the poll. e) Working into both reins on a circle correctly in balance. If the rider sits correctly and supports the horse with body and leg aids, the horse should work into an elastic contact.*

Exercises to Improve Contact

Exercise 1 (dressage and jumping)
Half-halts

A half-halt is correction to the horse's balance and obedience and its function is to ask the horse to take weight behind. The message the rider gives the horse with the half-halt is: 'step under me and get off my hands!' An unbalanced horse will lean on your reins and will need frequent and obvious half-halts to balance him. A balanced horse accepts a light contact but will need subtle, light half-halts as maintenance. The half-halt adjusts the horse's balance by asking him to take more weight on his hind legs, bringing them under his body, which lightens his forehand and is the foundation of collection. It also prevents his attention wandering and helps to keep him focused on his rider.

If your horse is working nicely balanced, not leaning on your hands, supple through his body and springy in his steps, your position will be feeling natural and your aids will be minimal. If this is *not* happening, you need to half-halt to adjust your horse's balance so that he can work more comfortably. If he is leaning against your hands, for instance, say 'step under me' by becoming braced or solid by firming your stomach and mid-back muscles (your core muscles), and by closing your thighs, knees and calves against the saddle. Close your elbows to your sides by pressing the base of your shoulder blades together. Do not pull on the reins, but do not give them away either: keep your hands and arms in the same position. Your back and leg aids 'press' or 'squash' the horse into the steady rein contact. As you do this, you should feel his back lift under the saddle, his neck arch, and his jaw will soften and he will chew the bit. Immediately you feel this, soften your aids back to normal, releasing the half-halt, but be careful that you do not collapse around the middle. Your core (stomach and mid-back) muscles must not slacken, otherwise your horse will drop his back and you will have to start all over again with another half-halt. The horse should respond to your half-halt by hesitating very briefly. As soon as you feel this hesitation you must immediately soften your legs, back and reins. All this happens within one of the horse's steps! Softening the reins does not mean loosening them: you should aim to maintain the lightest contact with the bit so that the reins are straight and soft, not loose and hanging.

A half-halt is not achieved by pulling at the reins, twiddling with the fingers and so on. *It is a body aid, not just a rein aid.* You should use hundreds of half-halts every time you ride your horse!

AIM

The aim of this exercise is to put the horse on the bit in the right way, i.e. from behind and not by pulling in the front end, and to teach the horse to trust the rider's hand and accept the contact so that he works properly through his back, arches his neck, and tucks his pelvis, taking weight behind. The horse should be brought into the rein contact from behind and not by taking up the reins first. The reins should only be shortened to take up the slack once the horse lifts his back and becomes round through his top line. (See Figures 3.5a and b)

Figures 3.5a and b *a)* (above left) *I am working Amadeus forwards from behind through the back into the contact showing how the horse should tuck his loins, and bring his hind legs under his body, and step confidently into the supportive rein contact. The horse's neck must be as long and arched as possible. Unfortunately riders are often seen hauling the horse in from the front end, which may make him appear round but he will surely be tense in his back and stilted in his steps. b)* (above right) *This horse has not yet learnt to work in canter into the contact and does not understand how to bring his hind legs under him, or to relax and swing through his back. However, after a couple of days of work on a long rein, using a light seat combined with rising and sitting trot, he managed to trust the rider enough to relax and work properly. Horses are not usually naughty; the problem is more likely to be stiffness or a misunderstanding of the rider's aids.*

THE EXERCISE

Place markers such as cones around the school in pairs so that you can ride between them. The pairs of cones can be randomly placed allowing you to ride a simple route involving straight lines and curves from one pair of cones to the next.

This exercise should be ridden in walk at first. Start by walking up to each pair of cones, halting between them and then walking on again. Next, halt between one pair of cones, and half-halt at the next pair, and so on. Then you could make the pattern more elaborate by half-halting between each pair of cones, and making transitions to halt en-route to the cones. Move on to working in trot and canter, half-halting between each pair of cones. (See Diagram 13)

WHAT TO LOOK FOR

What you are trying to achieve is a half-halt at a given point. You can use half-halts and transitions en route to each pair of cones, but try to achieve a really accurate half-halt when your knee is level with the cones. This is good preparation work for any competition: in a dressage test, for example, when you have to perform something at a

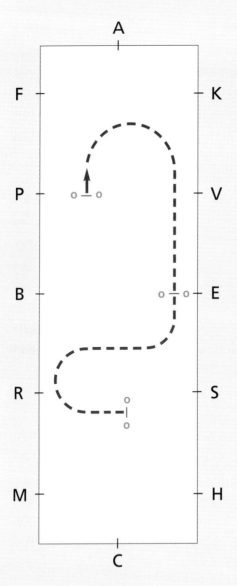

Diagram 13 *Exercise 1 Half-halts and halts at set markers, working the horse on the bit and through his back. This will also help the development of the rider's seat.*

given point, or when setting up a horse for take-off at a jump. Make sure the horse is straight when he is between the cones; this will make it easier for him to step under behind with both hind legs than if he is crooked. Once he steps under correctly each time, he should lift and arch his neck, and reach forwards to the bit, accepting your rein contact. He should be 'in' the reins, not against the reins. The reins are there to support the outline, not to create it falsely.

TRAINING TIPS
- In the beginning you may find it helpful to try this variation: walk between a pair of cones, ask the horse to halt, but then change your mind and walk on again. This gives you an obvious half-halt. The horse should hesitate and then walk on again. If he does not hesitate but just slows down then speeds up, this is not a half-halt and he has not taken weight behind.
- When in trot, try coming down to walk for one step between the cones and then trotting on again. Next, attempt the half-halt by asking for walk but changing your mind just before the horse actually walks. The message you are giving the horse is: 'I might walk, oops, changed my mind!' This gives you a half-halt in trot.
- In canter, the same thing applies. Keeping this 'oops, changed my mind' thought in your head helps you to get the most from your half-halts so that they are really effective in asking the horse to take weight behind. Only when he does so correctly will he truly be on the bit and accept the contact properly.

PROBLEM SOLVING
- If your half-halts do not seem to be working, go back to doing one step of walk, or a brief halt, to make sure the horse is stepping under behind properly.
- If your reins are too slack, the horse will not be able to chew the bit, as it will be jangling around in his mouth and clanking against his teeth. You need to hold the bit quietly against the horse's gums so that you can feel him chewing.

● If your rein contact is too strong, or you are using your reins before your body aids in your half-halts, then your horse will most likely raise his head and resist the contact. Make sure your body aids are correct, and ensure you are not tensing up your arms and shoulders, which should have the same body tone as the rest of you, or less when the horse is balanced. They should never be your strongest aid.

Exercise 2 (dressage and jumping)
Stretching forwards and downwards: seeking the contact

Allowing your horse to stretch is an essential part of training. If your training is correct, he should willingly follow the bit forward and down when you ease your reins.

Begin each training session on a long rein. It can help to walk him over randomly placed poles to help him reach down with his neck and loosen up his joints as he picks his feet up over each one. He will naturally look down at the poles, so stretching his back and neck muscles.

If your horse cannot work long and low, i.e. stretching forwards and down, when you first start your session, begin by walking him with a contact in a semi-stretched outline so that he is on the bit on a long rein. Acquire the feeling of the rein contact being attached to your elbows; this keeps your arms in a good position, and allows you to keep soft hands. Maintaining a steady contact will help him to reach forward into the reins. Use frequent half-halts – applied with your whole body, not just the reins – to lift his back and enable him to take more weight on his hind legs. Once he lifts his back, he will want to stretch his neck forward and down. Soften the contact as a reward when he responds to your half-halts, so that the reins feel like elastic bands. Letting the contact go too much too soon may surprise him and result in him rushing forward on his forehand. When he is in balance, he should reach for the bit as you lengthen the reins.

Support him with your body by remaining in a good, upright position, with toned tummy, back and leg muscles, so that he is not relying on your reins for support before you work him deeper. If he usually relies on the reins when ridden in an outline, he will feel all at sea when the reins are loose. Keep checking your own position in order to maintain your own balance. When he is correctly balanced, he should feel as though he is in four-wheel drive as opposed to front-wheel drive!

Riding in a slower rhythm on large circles will help. Mark these out with poles placed in a large star shape (see Diagram 1, exercise 1b in Rhythm, page 35). Keep your lower leg on to keep the impulsion, and use your thighs and upper body to hold him and prevent him going faster. His stride will feel more springy and slow when working in balance. Once you feel him lift his back underneath your seat, now is the time to stretch him deeper. Think of trying to push his nose down and away from you with the reins. When he stretches down in walk proceed to the same thing in trot, and then in canter.

Work for about ten to fifteen minutes at a time on your transitions, to enable your horse to take more weight on his hind legs, and then ease the contact so that he is on a longer rein, but still working through his back into the bridle. Each time you feel him lose balance, correct him either with a half-halt or two or, if this does not work, a downward transition. He should be stretching with his nose going down to the ground. Stretch your horse at frequent intervals, not necessarily just at the beginning and end of work, so that he gains the confidence to stretch lower each time, and is happy to be brought back into a more collected, rounder outline without concertina-like tension through his back!

AIM

The aim of this exercise is to encourage the horse to 'seek the bit' and to *Die Züegel aus der Hand kauen lassen*, which, in English, means to 'chew the reins out of the rider's hand'. In other words, the horse should stretch forwards and down while still accepting a soft contact with the rider's hands, chewing quietly on the bit as he does so. The key to this is the chewing aspect. If the rider just drops the reins, then the horse will no longer be chewing, and the reins will be floppy, i.e. there will be no contact. Hauling the bit, or even the horse's neck, from side to side to make the horse drop his neck also kills off any willingness to chew. He may well drop his neck, but will do so to avoid the bit and will more than likely come behind the bit, and who would blame him! (This is all too common in training and competition these days, unfortunately.)

THE EXERCISE

Ride a large circle at one end of the school with the horse stretching forwards and downwards. This circle can be 20m or 15m in diameter. At the other end of the school ride a second circle the same size as the first, but this time with the horse on the bit. Alternate between the two circles. Initially you may wish to ride each circle two or three times to ensure that your horse works properly, first stretching and then on the bit, but aim to do one circle of each eventually. Make sure you work the horse equally on both reins. The exercise can be ridden in walk, trot and canter. (See Diagram 14)

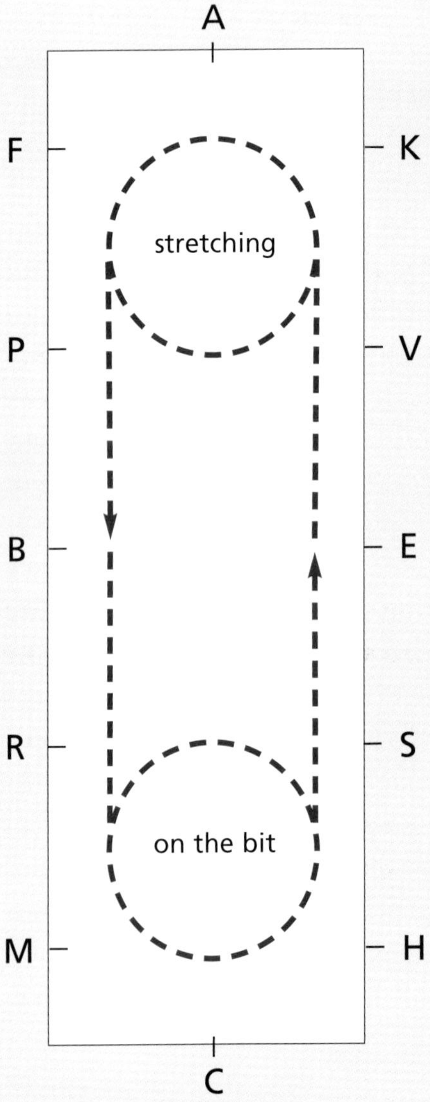

WHAT TO LOOK FOR

The horse should remain in rhythm, be loose and relaxed, and able to change easily from working on the bit to stretching with ease and without resistance to your aids. He should be quietly chewing at the bit at all times. You should be able to achieve this in walk, trot and canter.

TRAINING TIPS

● You could take the exercise to a higher level by riding different gaits both stretching forwards and down, and on the

Diagram 14 *Exercise 2 Using 15m or 20m circles at both ends of the school with the horse stretching around one circle and working on the bit around the other.*

bit, for example: medium walk stretching with collected walk on the bit; collected trot on the bit, followed by collected trot with a stretch; or medium canter on the bit, with collected canter with a stretch, and so on. This is a real test of balance for the horse and for the rider's aids!

- Use the straight lines connecting the two circles to make sure you are riding the horse in position properly, which will prepare him for the next circle. The better the horse's balance and straightness, the better he will be able to stretch, and work on the bit.
- Use frequent half-halts to ensure that the horse is working properly from behind at all times.

PROBLEM SOLVING

- If your horse is reluctant to stretch under saddle, do some work on the lunge and over ground poles to help him to loosen up through his back (see Suppleness, page 61). You could also do some work in a light seat with your weight on your stirrups and not on the horse's back to help him to relax and stretch.
- If your horse finds it difficult to come up onto the bit after stretching, then you must correct your aids. Make sure you are keeping the horse balanced with your position and body aids – a combination of your back, hips, legs and arms (i.e. half-halts). If you are relying too much on the reins to lift the horse's neck, then he will be tight in his back, and not be working from behind. The horse's back must be lifted in order for him to raise his neck.
- If your horse loses balance when going onto a straight line from a circle, then make sure you have him working properly in position and reacting to your inside leg aid pushing his ribs in the direction of your outside hand. Check this positioning by softening your inside rein. If you can soften the rein without him losing his balance, then he is working properly. If you cannot, then use frequent half-halts with your inside leg placed a little more firmly against the horse to support him.

Exercise 3 (dressage)
Shoulder-in on a circle
(See Rhythm, page 21 for how to ride shoulder-in)

In Rhythm, we used shoulder-in on a straight line. For this exercise, we will use shoulder-in on a circle.

AIM
This exercise familiarises the horse with working in shoulder-in and into the outside rein correctly. If the positioning of the horse is accurate, then the rider should be able to soften the inside rein without the horse losing balance and rhythm.

THE EXERCISE
Start by riding the horse in position (inside leg to outside hand) around the school and then bring him into shoulder-in for a few steps at a time on the track. Once this is successful, bring him onto a 20m circle in position. Once this is correct, and you can soften your inside rein without disturbing the horse's balance, increase the angle of his body by turning your upper body more to the inside so that your hips and shoulders, and the horse's shoulders are in off the circle line (see Figure 3.6 and Diagram 15). Imagine you are riding shoulder-in along a circular fence. After you have ridden two or three circles, then take the horse in shoulder-in up the long side of the school for a few steps, before reducing the angle so he is in position again. Change the rein across the diagonal, straightening him so that he is working equally from both hind legs, into both sides of the bit. Make sure you are sitting level, with equal weight on both seat bones and into both stirrups. This exercise can be ridden in walk, trot and canter.

Figure 3.6 *Shoulder-in on a circle using ground poles as a guide. The forehand should be facing towards the inside of the circle and the rider's upper body should be in line with the horse's withers. Amadeus and I are both facing correctly into the circle, but I have collapsed slightly to the inside and my inside leg is slightly too far back. The inside leg should always be nearer the girth than the outside leg.*

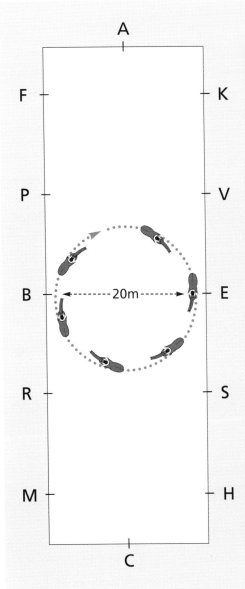

Diagram 15 *Exercise 3 Shoulder-in on a circle working the horse from the inside leg to the outside hand.*

WHAT TO LOOK FOR

The horse should step sideways around the circle, crossing his front legs, and stepping forwards under his mid-line with his inside hind leg. If you ride this exercise with too much angle and no bend in the horse's ribs, it becomes a leg-yield (moving away from the rider's inside leg at the girth) rather than a shoulder-in. Horse and rider should be facing inwards on the circle at an angle of 30 degrees from the circle line. Their heads should line up with the centre of their chests. The horse should be working into the rider's outside rein. The rider's outside leg prevents the horse from swinging his haunches out, thus ensuring that the horse has to bend his ribs around the rider's leg as he steps sideways. The rider should be able to soften the inside rein without the horse losing balance.

TRAINING TIPS

- A variation on this exercise is to ride half the circle as shoulder-in, and the second half as shoulder-out. This is very useful if the horse tends to drift to the outside with his haunches in the shoulder-in as it gains control of the wayward hind leg.

- Continue the shoulder-in on a straight line up the long side and then ride a second 'normal' circle, i.e. in position. This varies the amount of bend through the horse's body. A shoulder-in, especially when ridden on the circle, requires more bend through the horse's ribs than riding him in position, which is the first degree of bend. A shoulder-fore comes in between the two.
- Make sure you work the horse equally on both reins, and intersperse the circle work with some diagonals on a straight line, with the horse absolutely straight. If your lateral work has been correct, he should be able to work into an even contact with both reins, with the rider sitting evenly on both seat bones, and applying the same amount of leg pressure on both sides.

PROBLEM SOLVING

- If your horse finds it difficult to bend through his ribs on the circle, and swings his haunches to the outside to avoid stepping under from behind, just ride half a circle to begin with, then ride the second half of the circle in position, so that you are breaking the exercise down into smaller, manageable chunks.
- If your horse is leaning against your inside rein, then you need to use a firmer inside leg to ask him to step more under his body with his inside leg, transferring the weight from your inside hand to his inside hind. Use half-halts frequently to rebalance him. Remember: a half-halt says to the horse, 'Step under me and get off my rein!'
- If you find it difficult to maintain the shape of the circle, place a marker such as a cone in the middle of the circle to give you a focal point. Alternatively, you could lay poles out in a star shape and ride around the outside of them to give you an accurate circle. (see Rhythm, page 35, Diagram 1, for pole layout)

Exercise 4 (dressage)
Travers/renvers/half-pass

Travers, renvers, and half-pass are all ridden with the same aids, i.e. outside leg to inside hand. They are named differently because they are performed at different places in the school, and on different lines. A half-pass is travers on the diagonal. The terms used for this movement in other countries emphasise this: the German term for half-pass is *traversale*; the English translation of the Swedish is 'Travers on the diagonal'; in French, the term for this movement is *appuyer la croupe*, i.e. 'push the croup', and it would be qualified depending on the movement's direction, i.e. to the wall (renvers), away from the wall (travers), or on the diagonal (half-pass).

AIDS FOR TRAVERS

Firstly, you must be able to position your horse properly into right or left position, and have mastered shoulder-in. Only when your horse can work from your inside leg to outside hand should you start training the travers (haunches-in).

In travers, the horse moves sideways away from the rider's outside leg in the direction he is bending. The haunches should be pushed 'in' from the track or line of travel so the horse is bent around the rider's inside leg, rather like a banana. The following points detail how to ride travers.

- To bring the horse into travers on a straight line, the easiest way is to ride a 10m circle, and on the last step of the circle, when the horse's head is facing up the track but the rest of him is still on the circle, hold the angle with your hips and upper body.
- Your chest and your horse's chest should be facing outwards at an angle to the wall. Turn your head so that you are looking between the horse's ears.
- Half-halt at this point to keep the weight on your horse's haunches. Increase the pressure with your outside leg to push his haunches in the direction of your inside hand while keeping your weight into your inside stirrup.
- Keep a steady contact with your inside rein.
- Soften your outside rein to allow the horse to move sideways along the track.
- Sit equally on both seat bones in order to control the placement of both hind legs.

- The horse moves forward and sideways along the track. If you have the correct angle with the horse working on three tracks and with his haunches to the inside, you should be able to just see the horse's inside hip out of the corner of your inside eye.
- Your inside leg at the girth asks the horse to keep going, and supports the bend in his ribs. Keep slightly more weight in your inside stirrup.
- If you think of using alternate leg aids this should indicate to him to move forwards and sideways at the same time.
- Both reins should keep the correct bend through the horse's neck. The outside rein supports the bend, and the inside rein should be soft once the horse has found his balance.

TRAVERS ON THE CIRCLE

The aids are as above. As you are on a circle, the horse's forehead should be facing along the line of the circle, rather like riding travers along a circular fence. You should be able to see your horse's inside hip out of the corner of your inside eye. The advantage of riding travers on the circle is that it emphasises the need to make sure your horse is working correctly into your inside rein contact. It increases the suppleness, looseness, through his body. The steps must be rhythmical and even. If they are not, the horse is not balanced properly and you will have to make sure your position and aids are correct.

AIM

The aim of this exercise is to familiarise the horse with working from the outside leg to inside hand.

THE EXERCISE

Begin by riding the horse in position on the long side of the school. Then bring your horse onto a 20m circle, again in position. Then ask for travers as above. Maintain the angle of the horse's body with your body. (See Figure 3.7 and Diagram 16) After you have ridden the circle two or three times, work him around the school on straight lines to give him a break. Make sure you work him equally on both reins. This exercise can be ridden in walk, trot and canter.

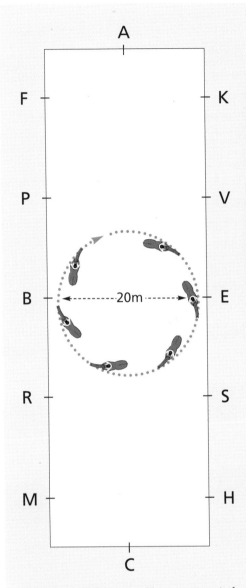

Diagram 16 *Exercise 4 Travers on a circle working the horse from outside leg to inside rein.*

Figures 3.7a and b   *a)* (above left) *This is quite a good example of travers on a circle. Both Heinrich and I are facing around the circle line and our shoulders are positioned correctly slightly to the outside of the circle. The inside rein is maintaining correct flexion to the inside at the poll. Heinrich's haunches are to the inside of the circle. I am asking for this with my outside leg, though my outside heel could be lower. b)* (above right) *Renvers on a circle but I have slipped slightly to the outside. My weight should be down into my inside stirrup.*

WHAT TO LOOK FOR

The horse should step forwards and sideways around the circle with his haunches to the inside. The angle should be just enough that you can see his inside hip out of the corner of your inside eye. You should feel each hind leg in turn taking weight as the horse crosses his legs. He should cross both hind and front legs as he travels around the circle.

TRAINING TIPS

- A variation is to ride renvers (haunches-out) on the circle. This can be very useful, especially if your horse is crooked, and moves his haunches to the inside as a way of avoiding taking weight behind.
- You could expand the exercise to include travers or renvers on the long side of the school, but make sure you work on straight lines with the horse in position to ensure he is correctly balanced.
- As with the previous exercise, make sure you test your horse's straightness at frequent intervals by riding dead straight across the diagonals of the school with both legs, both seat bones and both reins applied equally on both sides of the horse. The horse should take an even contact and work equally with both sides of his back, and with both hind legs.

PROBLEM SOLVING

- A rider leaning one way or the other disturbs the horse's balance and inhibits the crossing over of his legs. Make sure you keep your weight equal on both seat bones to prevent this happening. Keeping your weight into your inside stirrup is quite sufficient weight to the inside.
- If you have too much angle, the horse will stagger around the circle with uneven steps, losing rhythm. He will also find it difficult to bend in his ribs and will lose flexion at the poll, so you will lose his positioning. If this happens, reduce the angle so that he relaxes again.
- If your horse is tight in his hips and finds it difficult to bring his haunches in, firstly make sure you, the rider, are not tight in your hips! This a very common mistake; once the rider's hips are loosened and move in sync with the horse's back movement in whichever gait he is in, the horse will also loosen up.

Exercise 5 (jumping)
Grid work without the reins
AIM

This may sound a bit back to front, but the best way to learn how to ride with a correct contact is to ride sometimes without reins! Isolating the body aids helps a rider to focus on body control rather than rein control and emphasises the fact that contact is as much about seat and leg contact as rein contact. If the body is being used properly, when the reins are retaken, a rider will be more aware of how the rein contact ties in with the body aids, and its effect on the horse.

The aim of riding grid work without reins is to develop the seat to the extent that the position is maintained without a rider relying on the reins, whether they are dressage or jumping riders! This is all about developing an independent seat.

THE EXERCISE

Set out a grid of small jumps or cavalletti spaced at 3.5m (11ft 6in) apart to give a row of jumps with no jumping strides in between, i.e. a row of bounce or in-and-out jumps (see Diagram 17). The number of jumps depends on the level of competence of horse and rider. The jumps should be about 0.5m (1ft 6in) high. Start with one and then build up to two, three, four and so on, adding extra jumps or cavalletti one at a time. Some people say that you should not use two cavalletti in case the horse jumps them as a spread, but I have never come across this problem myself. If you are in any doubt about this, you could double space two cavalletti so that there is a stride in between (7m [23ft] distance apart). When you add the third cavalletti, place it in between the other two at the bounce distance of 3.5m (11ft 6in) again.

After loosening the horse up and riding some preparatory canter work, such as circles, transitions, and so on, in jumping position and in a light seat until both you and the horse are relaxed and the canter is bouncy enough to cope with the grid, tie a knot in your reins but keep hold of them.

Bring the horse into the grid in trot, and allow him to break into canter over the first cavalletti; then let go of the reins and put your hands forwards in the direction of the horse's mouth as though holding the reins. Maintain the canter through the row of small jumps with your leg aids, and remain in a light, balanced seat through the grid, folding at the hips as necessary over each cavalletti. (See Rhythm, page 21, for advice on the jumping position and riding in a light seat.)

If your horse does not mind you holding your arms out to the side, this is also a useful exercise. Concentrate on holding your arms steady as you go over the cavalletti in canter.

Take the reins again after the last jump so that you can prepare your horse for another attempt. Aim to do the grid three or four times in succession. Finish by retaking your reins and riding school movements such as circles, transitions, or some lateral work. You should find a big difference in the security of your position and the effectiveness of your body aids, hopefully resulting in a softer, more subtle rein contact than before!

WHAT TO LOOK FOR

You should ensure that your lower leg position is very secure, i.e. that your lower leg does not change position at all as you go over the cavalletti. Keep your knees on the saddle, and brace your thighs to keep you in a light seat. Your leg joints should 'hinge' to act as shock

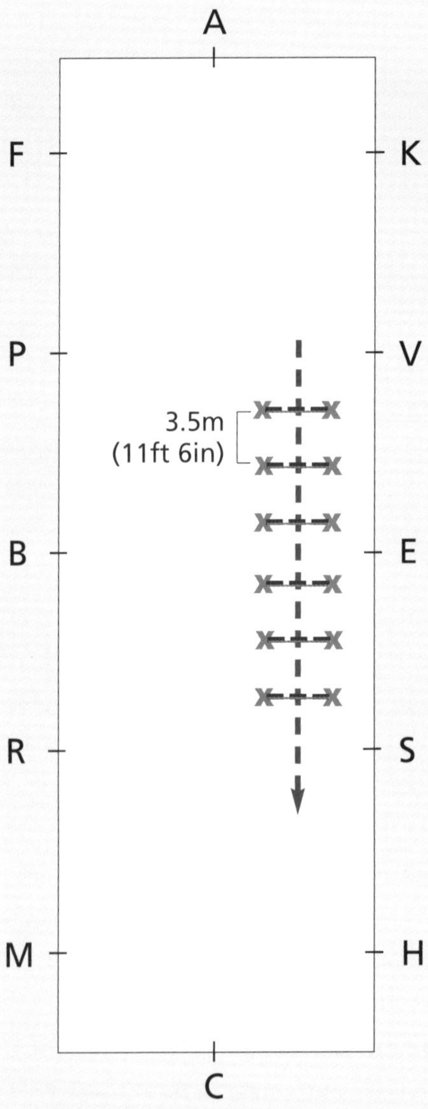

Diagram 17 *Exercise 5 Riding over cavalletti in the jumping seat, without reins, develops an independent seat.*

absorbers when you go over the small jumps. Keep your upper body toned as it is when you are sitting in the saddle – remember those all important stomach and back muscles; if you collapse your stomach muscles when you go over the jumps, you will find it impossible to keep your arms and hands steady, which will tell you that you are relying on your reins to keep your hands still! You should just fold from your hips at each cavalletti, keeping in balance with your horse.

TRAINING TIPS

- Make sure your stirrups are a comfortable length. If they are too long, you will find it difficult to keep a steady lower leg and your legs will tend to drift backwards or forwards.

- You can ride this exercise in a dressage saddle if it allows you to ride with short enough stirrups, you are just jumping low cavalletti and your horse is well-behaved! If he is likely to buck and get too excited, then use a GP saddle so that you can ride with your thighs in front of you, as opposed to underneath you, to give you a secure jumping seat.

- Keep your horse straight with your legs and hips after the grid and make a downward transition with him straight. If your horse is sufficiently on your aids, you should be able to make the transition without picking up the reins. However, if he is not paying attention enough, then pick your reins up, but do not over-use them!

PROBLEM SOLVING

- If your horse takes advantage and ducks out when you drop the reins, keep them for the first couple of jumps and then release them once he is jumping rhythmically. If necessary spend longer loosening him up and getting him responsive to your aids.

- If you are at all anxious, then you need to work on your own frame of mind before attempting this exercise. You must have trust between horse and rider for this exercise to be effective and valuable otherwise you will just frighten yourself and cause your horse to lose confidence in you.

- If your horse veers to one side when you jump through the grid, make sure you are not leaning to one side as this will unbalance him. You need to practise keeping the horse straight with your legs and body. If necessary, pick up the reins to correct him by straightening his neck if necessary, but then drop them again once he is straight.

Exercise 6 (jumping)
Grid work with a rein contact
AIM
This exercise follows on from the previous exercise, and teaches the rider how to maintain a steady contact with the horse's mouth allowing the neck to be used for balance. The contact should support the horse and help him to balance and maintain his outline, not restrict him and cause him to tighten through his back.

THE EXERCISE
Build the grid as before with a row of cavalletti or small jumps of about 0.5m (1ft 6in) high. Then place two other jumps of up to 1m (3ft) high as shown in Diagram 18, so they can be jumped after the grid on a curved line.

WHAT TO LOOK FOR
Make sure you approach the grid and the single obstacles straight with the horse working equally into both your reins. You will have to pick a good line of approach to

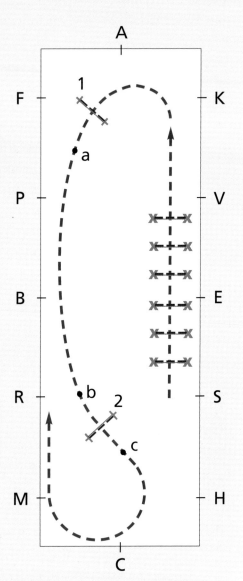

Diagram 18 *Exercise 6 Riding over cavalletti with contact and making changes of direction over jumps to keep a horse into the outside rein.*

bring you to the middle of each jump. Make sure you repeat the exercise on both reins. Aim at three attempts on each rein, take a break by riding different movements around the school such as circles or shallow loops or ride in between the single jumps, and then ride the grid and jumps on the other rein. Remember to stretch the horse frequently to keep him relaxed.

TRAINING TIPS

- Keep a steady contact with the bit at all times. Remain in a light seat throughout the grid, and make sure you maintain a straight line from your elbow to the horse's mouth via the rein contact. Allow the horse to use his neck as he jumps. The reins should be straight, not hanging in loops, and should be as soft as possible. (See Figures 3.8a, b and c)
- After the grid, pick your approach line to the first jump carefully, and make sure you ride your horse in position around any curved line to keep him balanced and working into your outside rein and leg. This will prevent him from dodging to the outside. Your inside rein should be softer to allow the inside hind leg to step forwards under his body as he turns.

Figures 3.8a, b and c *Jo and Trevor showing how the contact should be used when jumping. It is important that the horse's neck is not restricted in any way over a fence. It is the rider's job to get the horse to the take-off point in balance, to go with the horse in the air, and then to resume control after the fence on landing. a) (above left) Maintaining a light contact with the bit over a fence. b) (above centre) Allowing with the hands over a fence so the horse can use his neck for balance, especially on landing, but still maintaining the contact. c) (above right) It is far better to release the contact over a fence than to not give enough.*

- Once your horse has landed over the first jump (**point a** on Diagram 18) ride a curved line to the new line of approach for the second fence, which means that the horse should be lined up for a straight approach two strides away from the second fence (**point b** on the diagram). He should land straight after the second jump (**point c** on the diagram). To ride the grid in the opposite direction, after the second jump curve away and continue round the arena and come in to the grid from the other end of the arena. Make sure your horse is working equally into both reins on take-off and on landing over each fence, and the grid. Then you can be sure he is balanced and taking weight equally on both hind legs.

PROBLEM SOLVING

- If you get left behind, or lose your balance, release the reins completely so that the horse can sort himself out. Avoid hanging on to the reins to save yourself. It is better to grab the mane, or use a neck strap. Regain your position and balance as soon as possible.
- If you hold the reins too tightly you will tense your arms and shoulders and not be able to follow the movement of the horse's neck. This will cause him to tighten his back, and he may well hit the jumps with his hind legs. This in turn will affect his confidence.
- Turning too sharply into the grid or the single fences will just unbalance your horse. It may be a good idea to walk the course beforehand, placing marker cones if necessary to give you a line of sight over each jump, and the grid. This ensures you always look up and ahead when you jump, and not down at the ground, which will, one day, leave you sitting on the ground while the horse jumps without you!

4 Impulsion (*Schwung*)

The Desire to Go Forwards

Impulsion means 'the desire to go forwards'. The German equivalent, *Schwung*, sounds much more dynamic and fun! *Schwung* depicts energy, cadence (see Collection, page 174) a willingness to go forwards, and, most importantly, pleasure or sheer enjoyment. A horse with impulsion shows ease of movement, in other words his way of going appears effortless, and he moves lightly over the ground in a rounded outline – on the bit with the poll the highest point (see Figure 4.1). He should be responsive to the rider's aids and be easy to ride.

The horse who can move powerfully with *Schwung* and in balance into a soft elastic contact, develops the strength to work in collection and remain straight in his work. Conversely, the horse who is able to collect and take weight on his haunches has the power to work with impulsion. These two scales of training, Impulsion and Collection, go hand-in-hand, and you do not get one without the other!

Before the horse is able to work with impulsion he must be capable of working in rhythm, show suppleness (looseness), *Losgelassenheit*, and work into a correct contact. He must also take enough weight behind to work in balance: the early stages of collection. Asking a horse to go forwards before he fulfils the first three scales of training (Rhythm, Suppleness and Contact) is a recipe for disaster. If the horse cannot work in rhythm with *Losgelassenheit* and into a supportive contact, he will just fall on his forehand, out of balance, and pull against the rider's hands. The rider's reaction to a pulling horse must be to half-halt effectively to support the horse with the correct position: a braced back,

Figure 4.1 *Impulsion in medium trot. Amadeus is in a correct outline with his neck reaching forwards to the bit with the poll the highest point. He is showing good impulsion with both hind and front feet working equally.*

elbows closed to their sides and the legs closed around the horse's ribcage. Once the half-halt has transferred the horse's weight to the hind legs, then the rein contact must be softened so that the horse relaxes his jaw, chews the bit, and flexes at the poll.

Hind-leg thrust

Impulsion is the power of the horse and the thrust of the hind legs against the ground, pushing the horse forwards and upwards (*Schubkraft*). This thrust creates the period of suspension when all four of the horse's legs are off the ground. This occurs most easily in the trot as the horse springs from one diagonal pair of legs on the ground to the other diagonal pair (see Figures 4.2a and b). Piaffe and passage are collected movements, but they also require a lot of impulsion, or thrust, which creates the pronounced period of suspension, particularly in passage.

In canter the period of suspension comes after the leading leg (inside fore) touches the ground. During the period of suspension, the horse tucks his pelvis under, bringing both hind legs forward under the body. The outside hind hits the ground first to start a new canter stride, followed by the inside hind and outside fore, creating thrust. (See Figure 4.3)

The rider's canter aid is most effective when both hind legs are on the ground creating thrust.

Figures 4.2a and b *a) (above left) Amadeus in a good springy trot having just passed the period of suspension. b) (above right) Norman showing natural impulsion in the field. Here you can see the period of suspension in trot which occurs between each diagonal pair. The longer the period of suspension, the more cadence the trot is said to have.*

Figure 4.3   *Heinrich on the lunge showing the period of suspension in canter. This is the moment when a flying change would occur. The aids must be given just before this moment so that the horse changes legs in the air. I always lunge with the stirrups hanging down because it helps the horses get used to the stirrups dangling, and they do not swing about as much as people tend to think. If I have a horse who is worried by the stirrups, I remove them from the saddle.*

In the walk, there is no period of suspension, as the horse always has one leg on the ground and so the walk is said to be 'forwards' rather than 'with impulsion'.

Impulsion not speed

Impulsion should not be confused with speed. Forwardness should not be confused with speed. A horse can go fast without any pushing power (*Schubkraft*). Without *Schubkraft* there is no *Schwung* or impulsion. Many instructors can be heard bellowing across the arena at their pupils, 'Get him more forwards!' while the poor pupil is busting a gut with frantic pushing and shoving to get the unfortunate horse going at more miles per hour. This usually results in a stressed horse belting around on his forehand, leaning on the rider's hands for balance as his hind legs are paddling frantically away out behind without having any effect on the 'impulsion' that is desired. Here is a poignant quote by Waldemar Seunig from his book *Horsemanship*: 'He [the rider] develops impulsion and allows any resistances to escape forward, straightening the horse by driving the hind leg of the difficult side underneath the load without tightening up and letting this forward drive spoil neither his temper nor that of his horse.'

Natural impulsion

Natural impulsion, or willingness to go forwards, should be retained and enhanced by correct training. A healthy, happy horse turned out in a field will show natural *Schwung*, or willingness to go forwards, in his movement.

This forwardness has to be retained and developed under the rider and is the prerequisite of impulsion. The horse has to learn to carry the rider with impulsion; this requires the tucking under of the horse's loins and is different from the free impulsion shown without the rider, simply because the horse does not have to carry a load on his back. For example, if you are carrying a heavy rucksack on your back, you will round your back to take the weight. If you have nothing to carry, you will not need to round your back and will stand in a more natural upright posture.

For the horse to develop impulsion under the rider, the horse has to tuck his loins and flex the joints of the hind legs (engagement of the hind legs). This gives the appearance of the horse sitting down, which in turn elevates the forehand. This lightness of the forehand enables him to go forwards easily under the weight of the rider.

If the horse is rounding his back properly it is much easier for him to carry the rider's weight. His back muscles ripple or oscillate as he moves. If he is truly balanced, and all the work is 'going on underneath' with the hind legs working under the horse's body, then he should be easy to sit to. All too often, a rider can be observed bouncing around on a horse's back, saying: 'Oh. I have such a talented horse; his trot is so big and expressive that I can't possibly sit to it!' If the rider cannot sit to the trot, the horse's back is not swinging, i.e. his back muscles are not rippling, and he is not taking weight behind. The horse's back tightens to carry the rider's weight wrongly and to defend himself against the thumping of the rider on his back. His neck will shorten and either draw back with the poll high, but the underneath neck muscles tense, or he will overbend and come behind the bit because he cannot possibly round his back and reach forwards with his neck to the bit. This horse will find it impossible to work with impulsion, lose his willingness to go forwards and be punished with whip and spurs. His neck will probably be hauled into a 'rounded' (overbent) outline with excessive rein aids and a lot of pulling. Poor horse!

Nervous energy or true impulsion?

Impulsion should not be confused with nervous energy. A stressed horse may appear to work with impulsion but this is more likely to be nervous energy due to the stress. This is not the right way to train a horse. A horse suffering from stress will not enjoy his work and probably have a shortened career due to mental and physical burn-out.

Many riders are afraid of true impulsion when their horses show it, and tend to race around in a very fast trot or canter to work it out of the horse so that they feel safe in the saddle. Often riders work the horse with a very short, overbent neck that prevents the horse from working with *Schwung* and kills his spirit or *Lüst*, i.e. his desire, inclination or joy. They then need to work hard, often overusing the driving aids of the seat and legs and resorting to sharper spurs to regenerate what they destroyed in the first place!

Impulsion (*Schwung*) epitomises the swing through the horse's back, allowing the hindquarters to do their job and power the horse forwards. The horse has to take weight behind in order to work with impulsion. If this is done properly with the hind legs under the body taking the same length of stride as the front legs, the horse carries himself in an uphill outline into a steady, supporting rein contact. (This leads on to the development of collection. Hence the further up the scales of training you go, the more they all interlink.) There should be freedom of movement (looseness) through the horse's body and no restriction through the neck, jaw or shoulder.

Incorrect muscle development

Incorrect or uneven muscle development will affect the horse's way of going and his ability to work with impulsion. The first thing that will be affected is the horse's rhythm as the horse will speed up and become unbalanced instead of being able to propel himself forwards and upwards with a lightened forehand from hind legs that are under the body. Any issues that creep in when working through the scales of training mean that somewhere along the line mistakes have been made with the horse's training, and so if your horse has problems with impulsion, you need to go back to the first scale, Rhythm, and start again, filling in the gaps as it were in the horse's schooling.

Jumping with impulsion

In order to jump well and to propel himself into the air, a horse has to have impulsion (*Schwung*) and pushing power (*Schubkraft*) from the haunches. A horse that rushes into his fences has speed, but not impulsion. This horse will be erratic in the way he takes off and lands over fences and his technique will suffer as a result. He will jump with a flat, tight back, and raise his head, trailing his hind legs behind him.

The horse that can spring calmly and effortlessly over any height with a correct bascule (rounding through his back and neck) and land lightly on his feet ready to go forwards to the next obstacle has impulsion. If you watch an experienced jumping horse going over obstacles, he will appear to jump in slow

Figure 5.4 *Jumping with impulsion. Note the power of Archie's haunches as he takes off over the fence. The hind leg joints are deeply bent as they are carrying all the horse's weight at this point.*

motion, but because he is balanced and powerful and can turn easily, he will be faster against the clock than the horse who is constantly being driven at speed between fences and then hauled back for take-off at the jumps. To have impulsion, the first three scales of training must be utilised: the horse must be allowed to jump out of a **rhythmic** canter and in order for him to take weight on his hind legs and propel himself forwards and upwards, he must also be **loose and relaxed** (*Losgelassen*), and work into an even **contact**. (See Figure 4.4)

The Rider's Influence on Impulsion

Generating impulsion

A horse has to be excited and have *joie de vivre* in order to show true impulsion; something that needs to be emulated by the rider. A rider with no get-up-and-go will find it impossible to generate impulsion from their horse! There is a saying: 'lazy rider, lazy horse' and I think this is very true. We owe it to our horses to be fit and athletic if we are expecting these qualities in our horses. (See Figure 4.5)

Riders are often afraid of true impulsion and are only happy when their horses are 'trained' to such a degree that they mentally switch off and there is no sparkle any more. This is often mistaken for obedience. To generate impulsion, the horse must first of all be going forwards.

Forwardness is a willingness to react to the rider's aids, and an attitude of mind, i.e. thinking forwards rather than speeding up (see Figure 4.6). Forwardness is the precursor, and the 'baby stage', of impulsion. The horse does not have to be travelling at

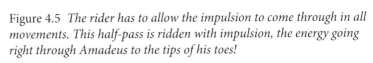

Figure 4.5 *The rider has to allow the impulsion to come through in all movements. This half-pass is ridden with impulsion, the energy going right through Amadeus to the tips of his toes!*

a rate of knots in order to be 'forwards'. A horse can be 'forwards' in halt by responding instantaneously to the rider's aids and waiting in anticipation for the next request. This is usually described as the horse being 'on the rider's aids', or 'in front of the leg'. However, anticipating the rider's aids before being asked is a result of the horse being almost too keen to get on with the job. I do not think this is a bad thing; often it is easier to teach a horse who is this keen and willing than one who ignores the rider and is mentally switched off. If the horse *is* switched off then he must be switched back on by intelligent use of half-halts and transitions and varied exercises to re-establish the rapport between horse and rider.

Figure 4.6 *This young horse is thinking forwards in trot and showing good impulsion.*

Legs not seat

Many riders are under the impression that you have to push with the seat in order to get the horse 'in front of the leg'. My question is what has your seat got to do with driving a horse forwards? If you want the horse in front of your leg, surely you should train the horse to react to your legs. It is rather like using a computer; pushing button A has a certain effect and only by pushing that button will you get the desired result. Pushing button B will just not work, however hard and long you try.

Leg aids ask for impulsion, not the seat. Your seat *accommodates* impulsion but does not actually ask for it in the first place. A tight seat is a blocking seat, and it does not matter how much you use your legs, the horse will not be able to go forwards if you have the handbrake on! Your back and hips should be supple enough to go with the movement of the horse's back and *allow* him to go forwards from your legs. As the horse's back moves more, so your back should move more, amplifying the horse's back movement, not suppressing it. Impulsion requires a *coordination* of the seat and leg aids. As the horse collects, your hips and back make a smaller movement, but allow the horse's back to lift underneath you. You have to sit up tall with toned core (stomach and back) muscles for this to happen; you do not want to kill off the impulsion. There is just as much impulsion required in a collected trot as in a medium trot. If you have no impulsion in a collected trot, your horse will not be able to extend, and tend to rush away on his forehand without lengthening his stride at all.

Forwardness and impulsion are generated by teaching the horse firstly to react to the rider's leg aids. A schooling whip and spurs may be necessary as training aids if the horse is really switched off, but initially the rider must make sure the leg aids are correct.

The leg aids

The simplest way of describing the leg aids is this: the rider's lower leg asks the horse to go forwards; the thigh collects the horse and lifts his back; and the knees are the brakes. The legs ask the horse to move. The rider's hips and back tell the horse *how to move*, i.e. they request a collected or extended trot, for example.

Let's start from the beginning and teach the horse to go forwards from the rider's leg aids. To ask the horse to walk on from the halt, firstly soften your thighs and knees (but keep them against the saddle, there is no need to stick your knees out) and loosen your hip joints so that there is nothing in the way of the calf aid. Nudge with both calves simultaneously, and at the same time be ready to 'walk' with your seat bones at exactly the moment the horse moves forwards. Your seat bones will move with the horse's back as he steps forwards if you allow them to, i.e. the horse will do it for you if you let him! Make sure you do not tighten your seat or push with your backside otherwise your horse will tighten his back muscles and not be able to move (the handbrake syndrome!). Once he walks forwards, keep your whole leg still for a couple of steps. Maintain a contact with your calves, thighs and knees, but there is no need to let your legs slacken and come away from the horse's sides. Think 'soft legs' not 'no legs'. The horse's reward for reacting to your legs, is that you stop using them but you should maintain a contact with your legs (See Contact, page 86). This prevents you nagging him with hundreds of leg aids that you do not need, which is just a waste of your energy and will only make him deaf to your aids. (Selective deafness is just as common with horses as it is with dogs – and husbands for that matter!) With the novice horse, you will need to remind him every three or four steps to keep going with a nudge from your calves. Once your horse is more advanced, you should only need to give him the occasional reminder; he should understand that he keeps going until instructed otherwise. As long as you keep your hips and back doing what you want the horse to be doing, he should keep going. If you stop moving, so will he. So, once your legs have asked him to move, your back and hips allow him to keep going.

If your horse does not react and go forwards from your leg aid you need to repeat the leg aid. If you get no response this time, give a quick tap with the whip, or touch with the spur, as back-up. If this *still* does not work, repeat the leg and tap aid a bit more sharply so that you do get a reaction from the horse. When he does go forwards, make sure you are not blocking him with tight reins. Teaching a horse to go forwards from your leg aid can initially be done on a loose rein, just to get the horse used to going forwards smartly. When he responds correctly, reward him with your voice and a pat, and keep going forwards.

Once he is moving willingly forwards, halt and repeat the aid to go forwards. If you achieved moving forwards correctly the first time and he understood what you wanted, this time he should go forwards when you soften your legs, a firm nudge should not be needed. Once the horse understands going forwards from a soft leg, your aids will become more refined.

To ask the horse to stop, close your legs: thigh, knee and calf, and stop your hips and back moving. If you stop moving, your horse stops moving.' In summary: 'legs on' means stop, 'legs soft' means go.

The rein contact should remain constant throughout any transition. The reins do not go slack when you move, or tighten when you ask a horse to stop. The horse must work through his back into the contact at all times for him to work from behind with impulsion (see Contact, page 86).

 ## Exercises to Improve Impulsion

Exercise 1 (dressage and jumping)
Changes within the gaits
AIM

The aim of making transitions within the gaits is to teach the horse to take weight behind and develop *Schwung*. Changes within the gaits can be likened to changing gear in the car, and you can put in as many gears as you wish. For example, you could have three gears in collected walk: 'extra' collected walk, normal collected walk, and forwards, or big, collected walk which is verging on becoming medium walk. Extra collected walk lies between collected walk and halt. It is the steps you get when you prepare for halt or for piaffe; it could be described as: 'half-halts in succession'. In trot, you could have three gears in working trot, i.e. 'small' working trot, normal working trot, and big working trot, which is verging on becoming medium trot. Small working trot has shorter slightly elevated steps but which are longer than collected steps, i.e. verging on the shortened steps required for preparation for piaffe. (See Rhythm, page 21 for the difference between changing tempo within the gait, and changing the gait itself.)

THE EXERCISE

This exercise can be ridden in walk, trot and canter. We will start with the exercise in walk, but just substitute trot and canter as you wish.

Using the long diagonals of the school, ride a 10m circle in a corner of the school at the beginning of a long diagonal in extra collected walk, i.e. collected walk with more engagement; preparation for halt. As you complete the circle, increase the length of stride to change the walk to normal collected walk. As you reach the centre point of the diagonal, ride a second circle in the same direction as the first in big collected walk, then continue along the diagonal line in medium walk. In the corner at the end of the diagonal, drop two gears into big collected walk. Repeat on the next diagonal, riding the circles in the opposite direction to the first diagonal. (See Diagram 19)

Repeat the above exercise in trot, riding the first half of the diagonal in big collected trot, and the second half of the diagonal in working trot. At the end of the diagonal, just before the corner, ride a transition to collected trot. (See Rhythm, page 41, for gear changing.)

When in canter, ride the first circle in extra collected canter (collected canter with more engagement) and on the straight line change gear into normal working canter. For the second circle, make a transition – change gear – into normal collected canter. The next straight section could be ridden in small medium canter (medium canter with more engagement verging on working canter). Finish the diagonal in big collected canter. When riding the exercise in canter, you will need to make a change of leg or a downwards transition to trot or walk at the end of the diagonal or on the short side. Mind you, there's no reason why you could not continue in counter-canter onto the next diagonal, but ride the 10m circles in true canter!

WHAT TO LOOK FOR

You should ask the horse to change gear each time you change from a circle to a straight line, and from a straight line to a circle, making sure that the horse is properly positioned and working into your outside hand in preparation for each circle. Make sure he is really straight on the straight lines, with the contact with your seat bones, legs, and reins parallel and equal.

Ride the diagonal exercise two or three times on each rein, and then ride up the long side in top gear, such as medium or extended walk, trot or canter to see how much pushing power you have developed. Drop a gear when riding the corners to maintain balance and to make sure the horse does not rush or get on his forehand.

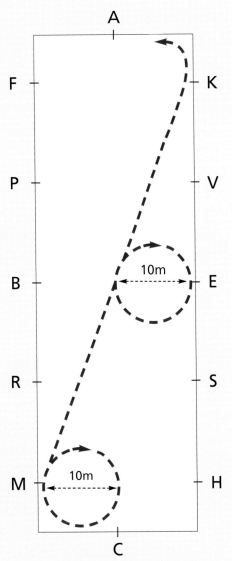

Diagram 19 *Exercise 1 Using small circles (voltes) to generate energy and then using that energy for medium/extended trot and canter.*

TRAINING TIPS

* You need to make sure your aids for each transition within, and between, each gait are correctly executed. The horse should be accepting the contact and listening to your body and legs. Both you

and your horse should understand what a half-halt is (see Contact, page 86), which tells him to take weight on his hind legs so he is not on his forehand, and thus be able to bend properly around circles of different sizes. It is important that you make sure that you are sitting up tall, using your back and stomach muscles to control him and not the reins, and to be able to stop and slow down by closing your legs (thighs and knees as well as your calves). Your hands should just maintain a steady contact with the bit so that he can chew quietly without leaning. He should not lean or feel strong if you have him controlled with your body. Once you can do all this, then you can execute transitions within the gaits smoothly and in balance.

- Instead of straightening the horse on the straight lines in between the circles, you could also keep your horse in position all the time, just changing bend and flexion at the end of the diagonal. This ensures the inside hind leg is stepping under the body all the time, and means that the horse is prepared at all times for the next circle.

PROBLEM SOLVING

- One of the most common problems that occurs when riders try to ride with impulsion is that they start pushing with the seat thus making the horse tighten his back. A good way to rectify this is to ride changes within the gaits in a light seat, which helps the rider to get the driving leg aids right without using the seat at all. It is important that your rein aids and lower leg position do not change. You can still half-halt in a light seat by closing your lower legs and knees and bracing your stomach and back, even though you are leaning slightly forwards.

- If your horse speeds up and slows down instead of changing the type of walk, trot or canter, then his hind legs are not under his body and carrying him but are paddling out behind. You will find it difficult to maintain each gait when changing from circles to straight lines, and vice versa, and the horse may well break out of trot or canter for example, simply because he does not have enough impulsion to take him through the change of gait. If you have difficulty with the 10m circles, make the circles larger and also work around the school, using the corners to give you the ideal opportunity to engage the hind legs. Each corner should be ridden as a quarter circle with the horse positioned so that he is working into the outside aids.

● If the horse leans against the contact for support and speeds up, this is another indication that he is not taking weight behind and you need to work on transitions from gait to gait and half-halts to improve the horse's balance so that he is not on his forehand. He should be working in the reins, not against the reins.

Exercise 2 (dressage and jumping)
Demi-voltes and reverse circles (towards the track)
AIM

The aim of this exercise is to develop engagement and improve impulsion by riding voltes (small circles) and demi-voltes.

THE EXERCISE
Exercise 2a

At the end of the long side, ride a demi-volte. This entails riding a small half circle of 8–10m, then riding back to the track on a straight line. As you reach the track, change the bend (position) and continue along the track. Repeat the demi-volte at the corner at the other end of the long side. (See Diagram 20a) This exercise can be ridden in walk, trot and canter. Ride two or three demi-voltes on each direction. Give the horse a break by riding around the arena with changes within the gaits, and larger circles.

Exercise 2b

Ride a volte in the corner inwards (away from the track) at the beginning of a long side. Then straighten, and incline from the track to a point 6–8m in from the track, opposite the middle point of the long side. Ride a second volte, this time towards the track, in the opposite direction to the first volte. Ride a third volte in the next corner, this time in the direction away from the track. As you complete the third volte, incline back to the track, so this time the middle volte is inwards (away from the track) and the third volte will be towards the track. (See Diagram 20b) Ride this exercise two or three times, alternating the direction of each volte. When you ride this exercise in canter you will have to execute a change of leg on the straight lines between the voltes, either a change of lead through trot, a simple change through walk or a flying change. You could change lead through halt if you wish: canter-halt-canter! Ride the exercise two or three times, then ride different exercises around the school such as changes within the gait, lateral work and so on. Always remember to stretch your horse on a long rein frequently.

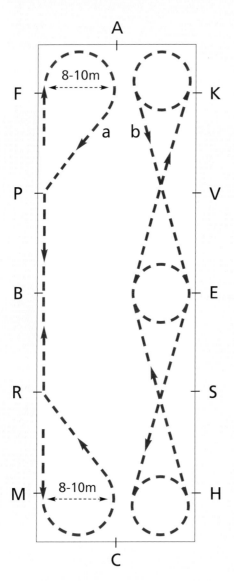

Diagram 20 *Exercise 2 a) Demi-voltes to improve engagement and b) voltes towards the track.*

WHAT TO LOOK FOR

When riding the voltes, make sure your horse is correctly positioned for each one and is bending round your inside leg enough so that his hind feet step in the tracks of his forefeet. Half-halt at each change of direction and change his position in the middle of each straight line to make sure he is set up properly for each volte. On each volte, your horse should step under behind and tuck his loins, rounding his back and arching his neck forwards to the bit. This should generate lightness, cadence, and looseness through his back. When you ride the straight lines, try to maintain this engagement of his hind legs to keep the pushing power (*Schubkraft*) between the voltes.

TRAINING TIPS

- In exercise 2a, the exercise can be ridden in walk and canter, using demi-voltes or large demi-pirouettes. With the latter, the horse must be able to take more weight behind. In addition, it can be ridden as travers in trot on a small half-circle, before straightening and riding back to the track, but be careful that the horse does not just put his haunches to the inside to avoid stepping under behind.
- In exercise 2b, riding the voltes towards the track ensures that they are accurate and a specific size. The rider has to turn accurately.
- The rider must be diligent regarding their own position and aids during this work to give the horse the best chance to remain in balance. It is so important to be self-critical when riding with precision.

PROBLEM SOLVING

- If the horse pushes his haunches in on the small voltes, make sure you have him properly in position at all times, so he is working into your outside aids, and he is not against your inside rein. You should be able to soften your inside rein if he is balanced.
- If the horse struggles with the voltes, then you can ride larger circles of 10–12m. Once he has the idea of how to balance, bend and step under behind, then try the smaller voltes again.
- Falling on the forehand or speeding up are symptoms of the horse not taking weight on his hind legs, so take a break from the exercise and work on transitions until the horse becomes lighter in his forehand.

Exercise 3 (dressage)
Lateral work on a circle
AIM
The aim of this exercise is to provide gymnastic work for the hindquarters and back, improving the horse's strength and power in his haunches.

THE EXERCISE
Ride a 20m circle, alternating between a quarter of the circle ridden in shoulder-in and a quarter of the circle ridden in travers (haunches-in). (See

Rhythm, page 21) This can be ridden in walk, trot and canter. Laying four poles in a star shape with their inner ends 10m apart can ensure the circle is accurately ridden, and the four segments are equal in shape and size (see Diagram 1). With this exercise it is all too easy to drift in and out without markers of some sort! A central cone can also help in place of the poles. (See Diagram 21 and Figures 4.7 and 4.8)

Figure 4.7 *Amadeus showing how much the front legs can cross when performing shoulder-in on a circle. My inside leg could be nearer the girth to maintain bend in the ribs. With a less supple horse, ride the shoulder-in with less angle, making sure the hind legs do not escape to the outside.*

Figure 4.8 *Amadeus performing travers on a circle. When working with impulsion the horse works through his whole body and puts a lot of effort into the movement. Amadeus is really trying his best! This is a great gymnastic exercise for the haunches and really loosens the hips – this applies to both horse and rider.*

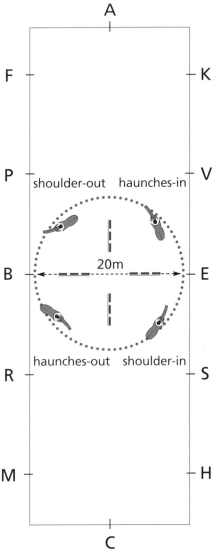

Diagram 21 *Exercise 3 Lateral work on a circle. Poles can be used to mark out four equal segments.*

WHAT TO LOOK FOR

The horse should be working correctly from your inside leg into the outside aids in shoulder-in, and from the outside leg to the inside aids in travers. You must change the horse from facing inwards on the circle in the shoulder-in to facing outwards in travers, without losing the horse's bend and flexion (positioning). This change of movement can be done over three steps to make a smooth transition between shoulder-in and travers. You need to keep the horse working from behind with frequent half-halts. The exercise should be ridden on both reins, and the horse given a break by riding around the arena on straight lines, with changes within the gaits.

TRAINING TIPS

- To simplify the exercise, or to give yourself more time to prepare the horse for each movement, the lateral steps can alternate with a normal quarter circle, for example, shoulder-in, normal quarter circle, travers, normal quarter circle.
- Ensure that you can do this exercise in walk before progressing to trot or canter as you will have more time in this gait to make any corrections you need to do.
- If the horse's steps are regular, and he is working in a steady rhythm, then he should take the same number of steps in each segment. The two segments of shoulder-in should have the same number of steps, and the two segments of travers should have the same number of steps. You may find the number of shoulder-in steps differ from the number of travers steps because in shoulder-in the forelegs will cross more than the hind legs, and in travers the hind legs will cross over more than the forelegs. You must maintain rhythm by making sure that you move your hips in sync with the horse's back movement. (See Rhythm, page 21)

PROBLEM SOLVING

- Too much angle in shoulder-in will cause the horse to swing his haunches too far out. Too much angle in travers will cause the haunches to step too far in. In both situations, the *Schubkraft* will be lost as the hind legs are no longer under the horse's body. To correct this, you must ensure your supporting aids are functioning to contain the horse's sideways, or lateral, steps.

- Too much bend in the ribs will disconnect the horse's back end from his front end, resulting in a loss of balance, and spoil the regularity of the steps (rhythm). Both of your legs must play a part in asking for and controlling the amount of bend. There should be a slight difference in pressure between your inside and outside legs. It is not a matter of all or nothing.
- Too much neck bend, caused by too much inside rein, will cause the horse to fall onto his outside shoulder in both lateral movements. The supporting outside rein should be used to keep the horse's head and neck in line with his chest. There should only be a slight difference in contact between the inside and outside reins. If the horse is balanced in the movements, you should be able to soften either rein to test the horse's equilibrium, or both reins simultaneously if your aids are correct and the horse is properly supported by your body position and aids.

Exercise 4 (dressage)
Demi-pirouettes and pirouettes
AIM
The aim of this exercise is to help the horse 'sit' behind and develop the energy and power (*Schwung*) required both for collected movements and for medium and extended gaits.

THE EXERCISE
This exercise can be ridden in walk and canter. Although there is no 'official' movement in trot, travers in trot on demi-voltes and voltes is very effective for improving the development of impulsion. (See Exercise 2a on page 129) This exercise to perfect the aids and accuracy of demi-pirouettes and full pirouettes should be ridden in walk at first. (See Diagram 22)

HOW TO RIDE A DEMI-PIROUETTE IN WALK
If working on the right rein, position your horse to the right. Collect the

walk with half-halts. As you feel the steps shorten and the horse's back lift, apply your outside leg behind the girth, and increase the contact slightly with the inside rein (as though you were riding half-pass) and lengthen your inside leg downwards, stepping more into the inside stirrup. This has the effect of anchoring the demi-pirouette on the spot. The smaller the demi-pirouette, the more you need to step down into the stirrup. The inside leg is used in quick pulses to energise the horse, to maintain the bend, and to make sure the hind legs step actively in rhythm. Your outside rein controls the speed of the turn but ensures that the neck remains in line with the body. Turn the horse with your hips, keeping your shoulders in line with the withers, and also ask for the turn with your inside rein. The smaller the turn, the more inside rein you need to guide the forehand round. Brace your back, pressing the small of your back forwards and upwards towards your breast bone. In the demi- (and full) walk pirouette, the horse should mark time with his hind legs, and the front legs should cross as he turns.

HOW TO RIDE A DEMI-PIROUETTE IN CANTER

The aids for a demi-pirouette in canter are the same as those for a demi-pirouette in walk. The difference is in the way in which the horse steps with his feet: the canter sequence of the legs must be maintained, as should the period of suspension. (See Rhythm, page 21) The horse's hind legs canter as though around a small plate on the ground. The front legs do not cross over but are raised off the ground in the canter sequence. Your inside leg maintains the activity of the inside hind and prevents the horse from breaking into walk or trot. It also asks the inside hind leg to step under more which creates more lift or elevation of the forehand.

Exercise 4a

Firstly ride your horse in position on the long side of the school approaching a corner. In the corner, half-halt a few times to shorten the walk steps so that the horse steps more under his body with his hind legs. Apply the demi-pirouette aids as above. After the demi-pirouette, proceed back to the track in a straight line. On the track, make a change of canter

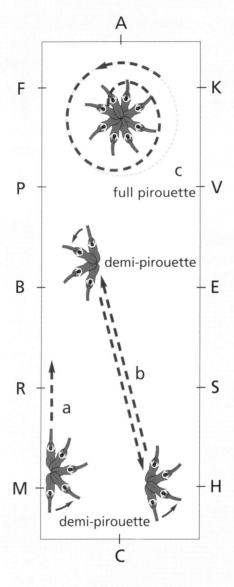

Diagram 22 *Exercise 4 Riding demi-pirouettes and full pirouettes in canter creates energy for medium and extended canter.*

lead through walk (simple change) or a flying change. Ride a demi-pirouette in the other direction at the end of the long side, return to the track as before, and change canter lead as before. (See Diagram 22a and Figures 4.9a, b and c)

Exercise 4b

Ride half-pass along the long diagonal of the school towards X, the centre point. The half-pass prepares your horse for a demi-pirouette. Make sure you maintain the horse's position (flexion and bend) throughout the exercise. Ride a demi-pirouette and then return to the track along the same diagonal line back to the corner resuming half-pass. Change position as you reach the track changing canter lead through walk or trot, or with a flying change. Repeat the exercise on the other rein. This exercise works equally well in walk as it does in canter. (See Diagram 22b and Figures 4.9a, b and c)

Exercise 4c

Ride a 20m circle. Gradually spiral in, maintaining the horse's position. Ride the smallest volte that you can with the hind legs following in the tracks of the forehand maintaining the inside leg to outside hand aids.

Figures 4.9a, b and c *A demi-pirouette in canter. The horse should have sufficient impulsion to be able to 'canter around a dinner plate' and must come out of the demi-pirouette straight and forwards. a) (above left) Amadeus is clearly turning in the demi-pirouette, but his poll could be a little higher. b) (above centre) The correct placement of the hind legs and a clear canter stride. c) (above right) Amadeus moving away on a straight line after the demi-pirouette – a good test of balance.*

Collect the gait, either walk or canter, with half-halts until you feel the horse take more weight behind. He will feel more uphill at this point. Ask for a pirouette (aids for the full pirouette are on page 191 of Collection): outside leg, inside rein. This exercise gives the option for demi-, three-quarter, full or double pirouettes and so on. The pirouette can be a 'working' pirouette, i.e. larger, with the hind feet working around a small circle. (See Diagram 22c)

WHAT TO LOOK FOR

The horse's hind legs must be under his body in order to carry weight. A true pirouette is ridden as a 'half-pass around a dinner plate'. Travers on a volte is just that; it is not a pirouette because the haunches are slightly to the inside which, in a pirouette, would be a fault. The hind feet should mark time on the spot as the horse turns. The forehand should lead the turn. The front legs should clearly cross over in a walk pirouette. In a canter pirouette, the front legs do not cross over, because the horse 'jumps' each step around the pirouette in the moment of suspension. Because the horse is, or should be, so much on his haunches in a canter pirouette, the moment of suspension is brief and so the rider has to be quick and clear with the turning aids, which have to be given just before the horse springs off the ground with the hind feet. The aid generates thrust, which can only happen when the feet are on the ground. As the horse takes weight behind, the forehand rises: the horse comes 'up' in front; this is the moment the rider turns the horse with their outside leg and hips.

TRAINING TIPS

- In Exercise 4a, using the corner to introduce demi-pirouettes gives the horse a definite place to turn. He cannot walk forwards, or escape to the outside because of the fence or wall, and so the only option is to turn in the direction of bend, or position, around his hind legs. The main benefit is that you remain relaxed, and are less likely to panic about the horse not turning as asked.

- In Exercise 4b, if you ride the demi-pirouette after X, you can repeat it to and fro on the diagonal, riding three or four demi-pirouettes in succession.

- In Exercise 4c, be careful as you spiral in that the horse's shoulders are leading and not his haunches. A pirouette is a half-pass on a turn, and not travers. Be careful when riding large pirouettes that they do not change into a volte or that the hind legs escape to the outside.

PROBLEM SOLVING

- Too much inside leg pressing against the horse will make the pirouette too big, and it will become a small circle, or volte, instead of a true pirouette. The rider needs to make sure they are putting sufficient weight into the inside stirrup in the right way. Ramming the heel forwards just stiffens the rider's leg by locking the ankle, hip and knee joints. When stepping down into the inside stirrup, the rider's leg joints must remain flexible. The horse reflects what the rider is doing so the reaction to the rider having a stiff inside leg is that the horse does also,

Figure 4.10 *Getting stuck behind in a canter pirouette happens when the forwards impulse is lost, and the canter sequence of legs is not clear. Here the hind legs are together on the ground instead of marking time in the canter rhythm.*

and the hind legs will tend to bunny hop together rather than step separately as they should.

- Getting stuck behind is a common problem when riding both walk and canter pirouettes when impulsion or thinking forwards is lost (see Figure 4.10). This can be caused by not using quick nudges with the inside leg at the right moment, which is just before the forehand lifts off the ground when the horse has three legs on the ground (diagonal pair and inside fore) so that the outside hind leg responds to the aid by coming under the hindquarters further. The other causes are: leaning forward, which puts weight onto the horse's forehand, or using too much rein contact, which blocks the hind leg movement.

- Spinning around with the hind legs escaping to the outside rather than turning on the back end is caused by the horse not taking enough weight behind to 'sit' in the pirouette. This can also be caused by the rider leaning forwards. The rider needs to work on walk-canter-walk transitions, or walk-halt-walk transitions, to help the horse to engage his haunches more. Making the pirouettes larger can help to keep the hind legs under the horse.

Exercise 5 (jumping)
Bounce jumps
AIM
The aim of riding bounce jumps, or gymnastic jumping, is to improve dexterity and agility. The agile horse can bring his hind legs under his body for the forwards-upwards thrust required to jump.

THE EXERCISE
Set out a grid as shown in Diagram 23 with the fences spaced at 3.5m

(11ft 6in) apart for a grid with no non-jumping strides. The grid consists of four obstacles: an upright followed by a spread, such as a parallel which can be jumped from either direction, another upright, followed by a second parallel spread.

As a warm-up, the jump poles can be laid on the ground and the horse ridden through the grid in walk, trot and canter. It is important to do this to check that the distances suit the horse. A horse with a big stride may need the obstacles spaced at 4m (13ft) apart. A pony with a shorter stride may need them set at 3m (10ft) apart. You could begin with three jumps – upright, parallel, upright – to accustom the horse to the grid before adding in the last element. This can be jumped in either direction and looks the same on each rein. Raise the last fence first, and keep the poles on the ground for the other jumps. Raise the other jumps one at a time, with the first jump being the last to be raised. The height depends on the experience and suppleness of the horse. Jumps should be set between 0.5m (1ft 6in) and 1m (3ft) with the width of the parallel spreads set at the same distance as the height of the jump, e.g. a parallel 0.8m (2ft 6in) high should be 0.8m (2ft 6in) wide.

Approach the grid in trot, and allow your horse to break into a canter over the first jump. This prevents him from coming in too fast and possibly frightening himself. Canter through the grid and make a downward transition to trot, and then walk in a straight line after the last fence. This ensures that the horse remains straight and balanced after the grid. You could jump the grid in both directions in the same training session, especially if you have a willing helper to alter jumps for you, or you could jump on one rein on one day and the other rein in the next session. If you are only jumping on one rein, make sure you ride the horse on both reins in your loosening up and stretching work. Aim for three or four successful rides through the whole grid on each rein.

WHAT TO LOOK FOR

The horse should approach the grid in a steady trot, maintaining rhythm and balance. He should be accepting the contact with the bit, and responsive to your aids. This should be set up in the loosening-up phase. If he becomes tense, crooked, or loses energy on the approach, then more

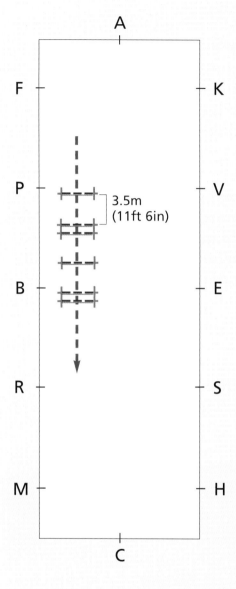

A

F

P

3.5m
(11ft 6in)

B

R

M

C

K

V

E

S

H

Diagram 23 *Exercise 5 Grid work using spreads and parallels at bounce distances.*

work is required on the horse's basic training using the previous scales of training before proceeding over the grid. Attempting to jump when the horse is unprepared will only affect his confidence in you. Conversely, if you are anxious, or not skilled enough to attempt a grid such as this, you should ride over poles on the ground and single fences until the basics of a balanced seat and clear, effective aids are mastered.

If the approach to the grid in trot is good, then a horse will have sufficient impulsion to break into canter over the first fence and maintain this canter through the grid. You must maintain a secure lower leg position, and be able to ride through the grid in a light seat, folding at the hips when the horse springs over each fence. Before the grid, you should be sitting upright in the saddle to bring the horse into the grid with his weight on his hind legs, so that the forehand is light enough to lift over the sequence of fences, and after the grid to maintain control over the speed and rhythm of the canter in order to make transitions to trot and then walk after the last fence. A light contact must be maintained with the horse's mouth through the grid, following the stretch and recoil of the horse's neck as he jumps and lands.

TRAINING TIPS

- If either you or your horse is inexperienced, then it is wise to use a neck strap to hold onto. This ensures that your upper body folds over each fence and prevents you from being left behind, and accidentally catching the horse in the mouth.
- Once horse and rider can competently ride the grid from trot, you could try from a balanced canter. It is wise to still make transitions to trot and walk after the grid to retain braking power. The more impulsion the horse has, the easier he will be to stop after the grid. If the haunches are under his body, and he is light to your aids, he should respond easily to half-halts and the transition aids.
- Keep the jumps at the same height through the grid. This enables the difference in the horse's bascule over the spreads and the uprights to be felt. He will jump shorter and rounder over the uprights and on a longer arch over the parallels. You will have to fold from the hips over each type of fence, and stretch more through the back over the parallels, in the same way as the horse.

PROBLEM SOLVING

- If the horse speeds up through the grid, ensure that your seat does not come out of the saddle, and remain close to the horse so that as the horse touches the ground on landing over each fence you can give a firm half-halt with the back, stomach and legs. Pulling at the reins will only make the horse stronger in the contact. The horse needs support and 'brakes' from your body. The rein contact can be used also, but the reins must never be stronger than the body aids.
- If the horse comes in too fast before he has even arrived at the first fence, the grid can be approached in trot or walk. It may also help to halt the horse on the approach a few steps away from the first jump. Wait until he is calm before continuing with the approach. It is most important in this case to halt the horse as soon as possible after the grid. Once this has been done a few times, he should stop anticipating the fact that he can shoot off over the grid, and instead anticipate the halt afterwards. In this case he will steady up on the approach in

preparation for the halt afterwards. Make sure the horse is rewarded for stopping promptly to your aids. It is most important that you remain calm at all times. Any anxiety or anger will transmit to the horse and just make matters worse.

● If the horse comes in too slowly or stops in the grid, then he must be ridden more positively forwards on the approach to the grid. The trot or canter before the grid must have enough life in it to carry the horse through the grid. Reduce the height and number of fences in the grid until the horse has become more willing and confident. More time may have to be spent on basic schooling so that the horse is more responsive to the aids, and treats grid work as a game rather than something to endure. A rider's attitude has a lot to do with this!

Exercise 6 (jumping)
Grid work with different types of obstacle
AIM
The aim of having a grid with different types of obstacle is to improve the horse's front and hind leg technique over fences, while developing impulsion.

THE EXERCISE
Set out a grid as in Diagram 24. Place three small bounce jumps no more than 0.8m (2ft 6in) in height, at 3.5m (11ft 6in) apart. The first two elements can be upright fences, and the third a parallel the same width as its height. Two strides after the small parallel, at a distance of 10.5m (34ft), build an ascending spread with the back rail 1m (3ft) high. The spread should also be 1m (3ft) wide. Of course, these heights and widths can be reduced the first few times of jumping this grid to make sure the distances suit the horse, and to give horse and rider confidence before attempting higher obstacles.

WHAT TO LOOK FOR
Approach the grid in trot and commence cantering on landing over the first element of the grid. Maintain a steady canter rhythm over all the

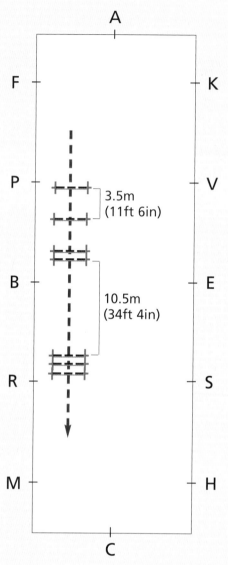

Diagram 24 *Exercise 6 Grid work with two upright fences and a parallel at bounce distances building up to an ascending spread placed two strides after the parallel.*

jumps. Keep a balanced position in the saddle, remaining in a light seat for the bounce jumps, sitting for the non-jumping strides and folding forwards into jumping position over the ascending spread. Sit up tall on landing after the last jump to ensure control and balance is maintained. The horse will alter the shape of his bascule over the different types of fence. You must be able to fold at the hip to accommodate each shape that the horse makes: more curved through his back over the uprights, and more stretched over the parallel. The ascending spread will require him to jump in an arc that is flatter as he takes off and steeper as he starts to come down after the apex of the bascule. The parallel will encourage the horse to pick up front and hind legs. The ascending spread will encourage the horse to fold up his front legs. (See Figures 4.11a–d)

TRAINING TIPS

- Make sure you have sufficient impulsion on the approach to carry you over the last element. You do not want to run out of gas before the ascending spread!

Figures 4.11a–d *Shape of bascule over different fences. a) Trevor taking weight behind on take-off over an upright. b) Trevor jumps in good form over this upright fence. c) He makes a big arc over this parallel and you can really see how much he lifts through his withers in the air. d) This ascending spread looks easier for him than the parallel; he makes it look effortless!*

- Learn to be proficient at following the horse's movement over each type of jump, maintaining a secure lower-leg position, and allowing the horse to stretch his neck as he needs to before attempting them all together in a grid.

- Ride the grid in one direction on one training session, and on the other rein another day. Allow time for loosening up work, and relaxing and stretching after grid work. The session should come to an end before horse and rider tire too much as it is then that mistakes are made. Always finish on a good note, even if the jumps are smaller than you intended. It is far more productive for the horse's training to jump small obstacles well rather than larger ones badly.

PROBLEM SOLVING

- If the horse tends to jump to one side through the grid, using cross poles can help to guide him into the centre of each fence, though ultimately it is you who has to ensure the horse stays straight by lining the horse up with the centre of the first element on take-off and keeping him lined up with the centre of each subsequent element of the grid. If the horse does not have sufficient energy to canter through the grid, then you need to spend more time on basic fittening work. This is not complicated, it can be as easy as adding canter exercises to the daily routine so that the horse can maintain canter for 10–15 minutes without stopping. This does not mean just cantering aimlessly around the arena; make transitions into and out of canter, and changes within the gait, i.e. gear changes in canter from collected to working to medium, and so on.
- If the horse rushes through the grid, then time spent on transitions is invaluable, especially canter to walk or to halt. The horse could be asked to halt on the approach two or three strides before the first element. The ascending spread could be set at a distance of 17.5m (57ft) to allow for four non-jumping strides, to give you the space to land over the third fence, halt or walk, and then canter on again to the last element. This is a very effective way of getting the horse to listen to your aids between fences, and not just jump in a gung ho fashion!

5 Straightness (*Geraderichten*)

The German term for this scale of training, *Geraderichten*, means 'to make straight'. Straightness is easy to define; the hind feet should follow the tracks of the front feet on straight lines and on circles. A straight horse works evenly on both sides of his body, and takes weight evenly on all four legs. A straight horse will take more weight easily on both hind legs as he is asked for collection. A straight horse will be able to perform a straight line up the centre of the school without difficulty, providing the rider is also straight! In practice, however, straightness is rather more difficult to achieve! (See Figures 5.1a and b).

In lateral work, straightness is also relevant. The hind legs should be placed under the haunches and carry weight (collection) and to 'push' the front end of the horse along. This pushing power, or *Schubkraft*, is an essential part of the development of *Schwung*, which we define as impulsion. A crooked horse has no impulsion and cannot work into an even contact. A straight horse works into both reins equally, keeps his ears level, i.e. the head is not tilted to one side, and will be able to bend equally through his ribs in both directions.

Most horses are one-sided, finding it easier to bend to the right than to the left. There are different theories as to why this may be but the most sensible one I have heard is that horses tend to be 'right-hinded' or 'left-hinded' with one hind leg stronger than the other. As riders and horse trainers, we tend to handle horses from the left side, and so it stands to reason that horse's become one-sided due to us influencing them

Figures 5.1a and b *a)* (right) *A lovely example of straightness with this young horse stepping confidently forward under his rider. b)* (far right) *Heinrich and I are making sure we are straight when warming up for a competition. If it is not right in the warm-up area, it certainly won't be in the arena!*

from birth. We generally mount horses from the left side because it became the tradition. Historically soldiers wore their swords on the left, drawing them with their right hands, and so mounting (and dismounting) from the left was the norm to leave the unhindered right legs to clear the saddle.

The crooked horse will tend to bend more to the right, move with his haunches to the right and fall onto his left shoulder. The muscles along each side of the neck and shoulders will be uneven in size: the left side will be thicker than the right. He will tend to lean on the rider's left rein, and avoid the contact on the right. His nose will be tipped to the right and the left ear will be lower than the right one. The horse will be stiffer, or braced, along the left side of his body and weaker on the right side.

Horses who reach the top level in competition and who stay at the top for many years are usually straight, i.e. they load all four legs evenly and work 'in four-wheel drive'. In dressage, there are far more competitors at the lower levels than there are at Advanced level. To sustain a career at Advanced level, the horse must be straight for the dressage movements to be performed accurately. At the lower levels of jumping competition, it is often the case that horses come into a fence sideways like a crab but will clear the jump mainly owing to their own dexterity rather than to any help from the rider. A rider who helps a horse by giving him a straight approach to the jump stands a much better chance of being in the prize money and having a long and successful jumping career.

A horse who is not straight runs the risk of injury. Stress is placed on joints that work too hard, and muscles become weak and waste away if not used, compounding crookedness. An injured horse who has not received appropriate veterinary and remedial care will become crooked to save the damaged part. This can become a habit and, even if the original ailment has healed, the horse remembers the discomfort and will continue to protect the joint or limb. Many back problems are the result of crookedness. Poor shoeing and foot imbalance can lead to joint problems and cause the horse to become crooked. Correct training and a high standard of horsemanship and health care is imperative for any horse to reach his full potential and lead a long and healthy life.

 ## The Rider's Influence on Straightness

Waldemar Seunig said: 'One must be either a very bad rider or a very good one not to be disturbed by crookedness'.

A bad rider will be oblivious to the horse's crookedness and carry on regardless with the horse making the best of a bad job and having his crookedness compounded by continually compensating for the rider's imbalance. Over time, this horse will develop uneven musculature on either side of his body, and be unable to work evenly into the contact. This horse will have a shortened career and develop physical and mental problems; any *Durchlassigkeit*, i.e. throughness (see Suppleness, page 61) will vanish into thin air. The horse is then often branded as being naughty or resistant when all he is trying to do is to communicate that he is uncomfortable with that rider on board. This can manifest itself through resistance to one side of the bit, going along sideways like a crab, rearing up, or even ejecting the rider with a well-timed buck!

If a rider is crooked – sitting to one side and unable to maintain an upright posture in the saddle – the horse will place more weight on the legs on the opposite side to which the rider is sitting in order to keep his balance. If a rider leans to the left, the horse will fall out to the right, and vice versa. A crooked rider makes a crooked horse!

A good rider:

- will be able to maintain an upright, straight and balanced seat, sitting equally on both seat bones.
- will maintain an even contact with the reins and be capable of keeping the horse straight with the seat, legs and hands.
- has sufficient physical strength to maintain the correct position no matter what the horse is trying to do to evade the aids.
- will read the signs that a horse is finding an exercise difficult and take time to straighten and correct the horse before things get out of hand and the horse becomes stressed, injured or upset.
- will distinguish between submission and mental switching off.
- will correct a crooked horse by not allowing the haunches or shoulders to escape to one side or the other.
- will control the horse's ribcage and keep the bit level in the horse's mouth.

Only a straight rider can give effective, clear aids to the horse.

Straightness will be affected if a rider is incapable of maintaining an even contact with the reins. In respect of right-handedness and left-handedness, a right-handed rider will naturally take a stronger contact with the right rein and be stronger with their right leg and the right side of their back; a left-handed rider will be stronger on their left side and with the left rein. If a rider is stronger with one rein, the horse's hind legs will displace to the rider's weaker side, e.g. a strong right rein will cause the hind legs to move away to the left, and vice versa. A horse needs the support of a steady, even contact to help him to work evenly through his body, and to use both hind legs equally. Crookedness at the front end is often a symptom of crookedness at the back end! A rider must learn to ride straight themselves. Physical exercises on the ground can be a great help to improve a rider's posture and co-ordination.

Simply not looking in the same direction as the horse can affect straightness. Riders are often told to look where they are going, but this is open to misinterpretation. To look where you are going when on a horse means that you should be looking between the horse's ears and look where they are going *now* so that you are looking in the same direction as the horse, with your chin in line with the middle of your chest. The horse's head should be in line with the middle of his chest. Most riders look where they are going *next* when they shouldn't be because this causes them to turn their heads too much and often goes hand in hand with the rider leaning in around corners, circles and so on. The rider then tends to turn the horse's head too much in anticipation of the next move by using excessive inside rein. A horse should be turned with the seat, legs and reins, not just the inside rein. Looking where you are going next without unbalancing the horse takes skill (see Figure 5.2).

If you need to look where you are going next such as when looking for the next jump in a course, you must ensure that your horse is between your aids, balanced and straight, so that you are able to turn your head without affecting your body position in the saddle and then line up the horse so that he is straight for take-off. (see Figure 5.3). How often do you see a rider approaching a fence on a turn with their head turned to

Figure 5.2 *Looking where you are going next without unbalancing the horse takes skill. You must ensure the horse is straight in order to do this! Rachel has a really good inside leg position and is keeping her pony Storm working properly into her outside aids. The hind legs are following the tracks of the forelegs.*

Figure 5.3 *The approach to this fence has been well planned; both Rachel and Storm are straight for the take-of over the centre of the jump and they are in line with the centre of the top pole.*

the inside and leaning to the inside, with the horse looking to the outside? This is often the case when the rider has little or no control over the horse's speed, and not letting the horse see the fence on the approach puts off the inevitable mad dash towards the fence until the last possible moment. This horse is not straight, unbalanced, and has no choice but to charge at the fence to get over it any way he can.

 ## Exercises to Improve Straightness

Exercise 1 (dressage and jumping)
Positioning the horse
Riding a horse in position, i.e. from the inside leg to the outside hand, is of great importance to the straightness of the horse. See Rhythm, pages 46–48, for details of how to ride a horse in position.

AIM
The aim of this exercise is to align the hind legs with the front legs so that the hind feet follow in the tracks of the front feet.

THE EXERCISE
Set out three poles in a line along the centre line of the school as shown in Diagram 25. This enables you to ride alongside the poles on either side. Lay them end to end with a 10–12m (33–40ft) gap between them. Leaving a gap between the ends of the poles can be a useful training aid: you will have to keep the horse straight or in position in an empty space without a pole to rely on! The next pole is a good check point to make sure you have not deviated from the line you were riding.

Alongside the first pole and first gap, ride the horse in left position so that he will be positioned away from the first pole. As you reach the middle pole, ride the horse absolutely straight. As you reach the third pole, ride the horse in right position so that he will be positioned towards the pole. This exercise can be ridden in walk, trot and canter. It requires a degree of collection (see Collection, page 174) for the horse to remain balanced and to take weight behind. The forehand must lighten in order for the horse's position to be changed.

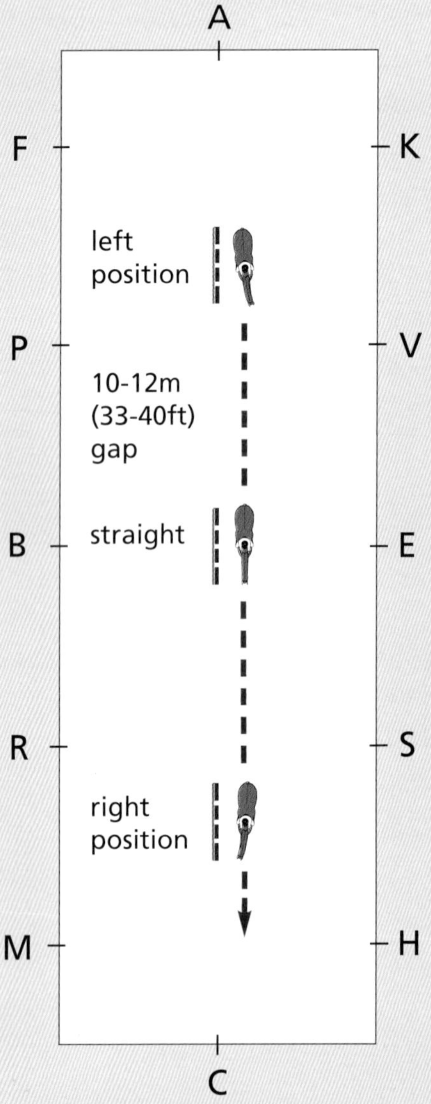

WHAT TO LOOK FOR

As you travel alongside the line of poles aim to keep the horse on the same line of travel. The change of position should be very slight. It is a change of emphasis of the rider's aids from left position to straight, and from straight to right position. The rhythm should remain the same, and the type of gait should remain constant. It is important that the horse remains relaxed and works on the bit in a correct outline with his poll the highest point.

TRAINING TIPS

- Half-halt as you change from left position to straight and from straight to right position when riding this exercise in

A

F K

left
position

P V

10-12m
(33-40ft)
gap

B straight E

R S

right
position

M H

C

Diagram 25 *Exercise 1 Positioning the horse. Poles are placed on the centre line and the horse is positioned left, ridden straight, and positioned right.*

walk and trot. This makes sure the horse remains in balance with both hind legs taking weight.

- When riding this exercise in canter, ride a change of lead through trot or walk (simple change) when the horse is straight. You can then progress to flying changes and tempi changes.

- **Flying changes** require straightness and it can be useful to ride them alongside a line of poles. The change of position should be very subtle. Many riders start flying changes by changing position sharply from one circle to another as on a figure-of-eight so that the horse has to change the canter lead to keep his balance, but he may well change late behind or not at all, becoming disunited. It is best to learn changes on a straight line to prevent this happening. Just keep a steady contact and concentrate on changing your seat from left canter (left seat bone forwards) to right canter (right seat bone forwards) and vice versa just before the up part of the canter stride. Your horse will then land in the new canter lead. Timing your aid is everything when riding a clean change and needs to be perfected.

- **Tempi changes** are flying changes in a sequence as opposed to single flying changes and require a canter with a clear rhythm and a rider with a good sense of rhythm also! The canter must be of good quality and the horse must be well balanced, light in his forehand, and strong through his back and haunches to be able to spring sufficiently at each change in order to change canter lead. Common tempi changes are those that make a flying change every four, three, or two strides, or every stride. The horse must have a very balanced canter and be able to collect easily without any disturbance to his rhythm. He needs a lot of bounce (impulsion) in his canter to do a sequence of changes, and has to be quite fit. You must be able to keep the horse straight, otherwise you risk swinging the horse from side to side at each change, and this can put you off course especially if you are riding across the diagonal! A line of ground poles up the school can help you to keep a rhythm and space your simple changes evenly. Start with tempi changes at every six to eight strides to give yourself time to get organised. Gradually decrease the number of strides in between each change, for example, ride simple changes, i.e. canter-walk-canter at four, three, two or one stride apart. This accustoms the horse to changing leg in quick succession, and gets you used to the timing of the canter aids. The smaller your canter aids are, the neater the changes will be. If you start throwing yourself about in the saddle, you will unbalance your horse. The secret is to have a really well-balanced canter with the horse straight and working with impulsion into an even, light contact. (See Impulsion, page 117)

PROBLEM SOLVING
- Sitting too much on your inside seat bone can make the horse unbalanced and he will no longer be straight. Always sit on both seat bones. Then you can be sure that both hind legs work evenly and under the horse's body.
- When the horse is in position, you should be able to soften the inside rein without the horse wobbling off line. If he does lose direction on straight lines, use more inside leg to maintain the horse's position and outside rein to support the outside shoulder and to keep the neck in line with the body.
- When riding in position, particularly on circles and with lateral work, bringing the inside leg back to give an aid or moving the outside leg from its place behind the girth only confuses the horse. The rider must be clear which leg is on the inside of the horse and which is the outside leg. Leg aids must be given where the legs are placed. This is particularly important when riding lateral work.

Exercise 2 (dressage and jumping)
Straightness on circles
AIM
The aim of this exercise is to make sure the hind feet step into the tracks of the front feet on circles as well as on straight lines. It also introduces shoulder-fore, which requires a little more bend than being in position. The horse is asked to bend slightly around the rider's inside leg and is the exercise to use initially to prepare for circle work and lateral work. The

Figure 5.4 *Heinrich demonstrates shoulder-fore; he is facing slightly to the inside with his forehand just turned off the track. You can see my inside leg keeping him moving along the track and asking for the inside hind leg to step forwards under the body. It is important that a rider's outside leg prevents the horse's outside hind leg from slipping away to the outside. This would result in a lack of bend in the horse's ribs.*

horse's inside hind leg tracks between the tracks of the forelegs, and so he is moving on four tracks. Riding shoulder-fore correctly ensures that the hind feet follow the front feet on circles and turns and the horse works properly into the outside aids. (See Figure 5.4)

THE EXERCISE

On the long side of the school, ride three 10–12m circles: one in the corner at the beginning of the long side, one halfway down, and one at the end in the last corner (see Diagram 26). The circles should be of the same size to help you with consistency of bend. Between the circles, ride the horse in shoulder-fore.

WHAT TO LOOK FOR

Starting on the right rein the horse should be positioned to the right on the short side of the arena before commencing a 10m circle in the corner at the beginning of the long side so that you and the horse are prepared for the circle. To start the circle just after K, ask with nudges with your outside leg for the horse to leave the track and turn your upper body, and head, onto the line of the circle. The horse should also be looking ahead onto the line of the circle. Your inside leg presses the horse at the girth to maintain activity and supports the bend in the horse's ribs. Your inside rein prevents the horse from looking to the outside, but you should be able to soften the inside rein at any time if your horse is working properly into your outside aids. On each of the 10m circles, the horse's hind feet should step into the tracks of the front feet. (See Figures 5.5a and b)

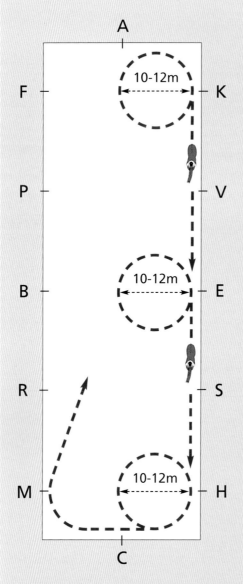

Diagram 26 *Exercise 2 Ride three circles on the long side of the school at K, E and H and ride shoulder-fore in between the circles. Change the rein across the diagonal M to K to repeat the exercise.*

As you complete the first circle, ask for shoulder-fore. Come off the circle maintaining the horse's position, then turn your hips and shoulders as one unit so that you and your horse are facing slightly to the inside of the track. Your thighs and calves ensure that the horse turns his middle with you to bring his shoulders slightly to the inside away from the wall or fence of the arena. Ask him to travel slightly sideways by nudging him with your inside calf. Your outside rein prevents him wandering off the track, maintaining the line of travel.

After the first circle ride in shoulder-fore to just before E and then commence the second circle as you did the first one. If the shoulder-fore is correct, then the horse will be straight on the circle. After this circle, ride shoulder-fore along the track to the starting point of the third circle just before H approaching the last corner of the long side. Ride the third circle in the same way as the others. After the circle, ride the last corner of the long side and across the short side in position. Change the rein across the diagonal of the school from M to K keeping the horse absolutely straight across the diagonal and then repeat the exercise on the left rein.

Figures 5.5a and b *Positioning to the inside on a circle. a) (top right) Heinrich in inside position showing slight flexion to the inside at the poll with the hind feet following in the tracks of the front feet so that the horse is straight on the line of the circle. b) (bottom right) As corners should be ridden as a quarter of a circle the same positioning and accuracy applies. Jo and Trevor performing an accurate corner in a dressage test with the hind legs following in the tracks of the front legs through the turn.*

Reposition the horse at the end of the diagonal in preparation for the corner. This exercise can be ridden in walk, trot and canter.

TRAINING TIPS

- Use half-halts frequently during the exercise to maintain the horse's balance, particularly as you change from the circles to the shoulder-fore and vice versa.

- Make sure you ride both sides of the horse, i.e. sit on both seat bones and use both legs and both hands. Using too much of one seat bone, one leg or one rein will make the horse crooked.

- The difference between inside aids (on the inside of the bend of the horse) and the outside aids (on the outside of the bend of the horse) is minimal. Any extreme differences will cause crookedness. The horse should be channelled between the inside and outside aids on circles and straight lines, as if he is going through a tunnel.

- It is most important to sit up tall all the time, especially when riding circles. Ride as though you have four columns around your torso, two at the front and two at the back. Your columns must never crumble or collapse!

- If you turn your head too much and are looking into the circle instead of around the circle, then your horse will fall in. Your chin should always be in line with the mid-line of your body, and your horse's head in line with the middle of his chest. Then you will remain in balance with your horse in four-wheel drive.

PROBLEM SOLVING

- If your horse tips his head to one side, use half-halts to make sure he is working with weight evenly on both hind legs. An uneven contact is a symptom of hind legs that are taking uneven weight. Make sure you are sitting on both seat bones and not leaning in, and that the horse is working with his poll level. Keep the bit level by making sure your elbows are equally placed on both sides of your body, and hands are equidistant either side of the withers. Taking emergency action by lifting one hand or taking one hand out to the side usually compounds the crookedness as the horse will go against a strong rein aid. You have to be able to maintain an upright, balanced position with every part of your body, blocking any deviations that the horse may try. The horse's easiest option must be to be level at the poll and even in the rein contact.

- You often hear the expression 'weight to the inside'; this means a little more pressure should be put on the inside stirrup and that is all that is necessary for turns, circles and lateral work. You do not need to lean in or sit to the inside. Leaning in will overload the inside hind leg, and it will not be able to step forwards under the horse's centre of gravity. If the inside hind leg is overloaded, the horse will swing his haunches out, bringing the loaded inside leg across his mid-line avoiding stepping forwards with it to track up with his inside foreleg. The unloaded leg, the outside hind, will escape to the outside. This scenario is very likely to happen on the left rein if the horse is 'left-hinded' and has a weak right hind leg. The right hind will escape to the outside and let the left hind take the load.

- If your horse puts his haunches to the inside on a circle to avoid taking weight with his inside hind, then this is likely to be his weaker hind leg, the one that avoids taking weight. This is most common on the right rein. The outside hind leg, the left one, will be placed across the mid-line of the horse to the inside to take the load off the right hind leg. The remedy is to bring the horse's forehand to the inside to line up with the hind legs by turning your hips and upper body more to the inside, and using both reins and more inside leg (pushing the ribs outwards so the inside hind comes under the horse's body) to bring the forehand to the inside. Once the horse is straight, the inside rein should soften.

Exercise 3 (dressage)
Serpentines in position
AIM

The aim of this exercise is to develop the ability to work in position on serpentines. The first example requires a change of position when crossing the centre line. The second example maintains the same position throughout the serpentine, the aim being to improve the horse's balance and coordination – and the rider's! It introduces working in counter-position (counter-flexion), and helps to improve the horse's ability to work from both hind legs, using both sides of his back and into both reins. The straighter the horse, the easier these exercises become.

THE EXERCISE
Exercise 3a

We will start with the horse on the left rein preparing to ride a three-loop serpentine. On the short side of the arena, position the horse to the left. Commence the serpentine at A, the mid-point of the short side. Ride the first loop of the serpentine as half a 20m circle touching the track for one step at P. Ride the horse across the centre line, keeping him absolutely straight for a few steps. After the centre line, position him to the right in readiness for the second loop, again a half circle of 20m diameter the apex of the loop touching the track at E. Cross the centre line again straightening for a few steps, re-position the horse to the left, and ride the third and final loop touching the track at R. The serpentine finishes at C. This exercise can be ridden in walk, trot and canter, though if riding it in canter you will need to make a change of leg through trot, walk or a flying change on the straight part as you cross the centre line. Ride the serpentine on both reins.

Exercise 3b

A variation on the serpentine is to maintain the same position throughout, which introduces the horse to counter-flexion (counter-position).

Commencing on the left rein once again ride the same serpentine as above, but without straightening and changing position as you cross the centre line. As a result of this the first and third loops will be in true flexion (to the inside), and the middle loop will be in counter-flexion (to the outside). This a good test for the rider in maintaining position and balance in counter-flexion. This exercise can be ridden in walk, trot and canter. Ride the exercise on both reins.
(See Diagram 27)

WHAT TO LOOK FOR

The horse should be working into your outside aids on each loop whether you are in true flexion or counter-flexion. Use your inside leg at the girth to ask him to bend his body and to step into the outside rein. The inside rein should be soft if the horse is properly balanced. It is very important to remember that the inside aids are on the inside of the bend of the horse and the outside aids are on the outside of the bend of the horse, especially when working in counter-flexion (counter-position).

TRAINING TIPS

- If you are riding in a short arena (20m x 40m) the loops will be 15m in diameter.

Diagram 27 *Exercise 3 Serpentines in position. a) Changing bend (position) over the centre line. b) Maintaining the same position (counter-flexion).*

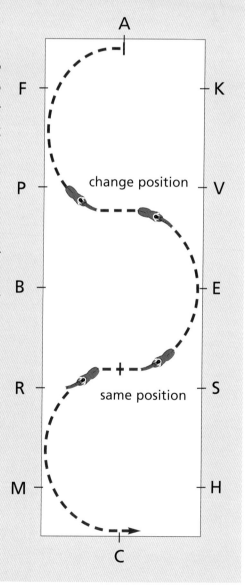

- Before and after the serpentine, make sure you ride properly into the corner before A and after C. Serpentines have no corners but are a series of loops, so make sure your loops are part of a 20m, or 15m, circle. Each loop, which should be a curved line, should touch the track for just one step.
- Each time you cross the centre line with the horse straight, half-halt to make sure he remains in balance in preparation for the next loop and change of position. He must keep his weight on his haunches so that he is light enough through his forehand to be manoeuvrable and able to turn easily in the new direction.

PROBLEM SOLVING

- When you are crossing the centre line straight and before changing position, make sure you are sitting straight in the saddle and check that you have even weight in both stirrups, an even contact in both reins and on both seat bones, and that your upper body is upright and you are looking between the horse's ears.
- If you collapse at the waist and lean to one side this will cause the horse's haunches and/or shoulders to drift one way or the other.
- If you lean to the inside when riding the loops, the horse will probably fall out through the shoulder, so the hind feet no longer follow the tracks of the front feet, i.e. your horse is no longer straight and he will not be able to make a good turn onto a straight line. Conversely, if you lean outwards, he may fall inwards.
- If your rein contact is uneven the horse will not be straight. Though the outside rein plays a supporting role and should be slightly firmer than the inside rein, there should be only a minimal difference between the two. Excessive use of either the inside or outside rein will affect the straightness of the hindquarters and the horse will go around the loops sideways like a crab.
- If your leg pressure is uneven the horse will not be straight. Excessive use of the inside or outside leg will cause the horse's body to swing one way or the other, leaving the hind legs trailing to one side and not tracking the prints of the forefeet.

Exercise 4 (dressage)
Loops
AIM

The aim of this exercise is to maintain the horse's position while using lateral movements. Single loops can be ridden with changes of bend from leg-yield (left position) to leg-yield (right position) or from half-pass left to half-pass right. Loops can be ridden without changing position either from leg-yield to half-pass or from half-pass to leg-yield. Lateral work improves the horse's suppleness and straightness because it improves a horse's flexibility in both directions.

THE EXERCISE
Exercise 4a

On the left rein, as you pass A, position your horse to the outside. By the time you reach F you should be in counter-position to the right. Leg-yield towards X. The loop can be as shallow or as deep (nearer X) as you wish to make it. The deeper the loop, the more sideways your horse should step, i.e. he should cross his legs more. Once you reach the mid-point of the loop, half-halt and ride half-pass back to the track aiming towards M. This exercise

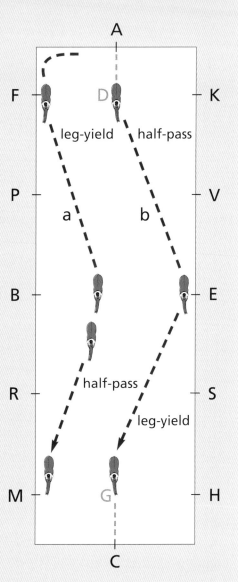

Diagram 28 *Exercise 4 Loops. a) Loops ridden from leg-yield to half-pass, maintaining the same position. b) Loops ridden from half-pass to leg-yield, changing position.*

can be ridden in walk, trot or canter. Ride the exercise on both reins. (See Diagram 28a and Figures 5.6a, b and c)

Figures 5.6a, b and c *Riding loops from leg-yield to half-pass, maintaining position.*
a) (above left) Amadeus in a leg-yield away from the track. My inside leg asks for the leg-yield away from the track so the horse steps into the outside rein. The inside leg must remain near the girth otherwise the horse will become confused when asked for half-pass. b) (above centre) Half-halt and change of direction ready for half-pass. Note that both my legs are asking the horse to lift his middle in the half-halt. c) (above right) Amadeus now returns to the track in half-pass. Note that the same bend is maintained throughout the loop and my leg position has not altered. The outside leg is asking the horse to step into the inside rein.

Exercise 4b

On the left rein, turn up the centre line at A and position your horse to the left. Starting from D (between F and K), ride half-pass left towards E (outside leg to inside rein). Once you reach the mid-point of the loop at E, half-halt, change your aids to inside leg to outside hand without changing bend or your position, and leg-yield back to the centre line at G (between M and H). This exercise can be ridden in walk, trot and canter but when in canter you will have to ride a change of leg through walk, trot or canter on the straight section between the half-passes. Ride the exercise on both reins. (See Diagram 28b and Figures 5.7a, b and c)

Figures 5.7a, b and c   *a) (above left) Amadeus in half-pass away from the centre line. The rider's outside leg is asking him to step sideways into the half-pass. b) (above centre) Half-halt and change of direction. Both the rider's legs are asking the horse to lift his middle enabling him to step under behind. c) (above right) Leg-yield back to the centre line. Note the same bend is maintained throughout the loop. The rider's inside leg is asking Amadeus to step into the outside rein.*

WHAT TO LOOK FOR

The horse's position should remain constant when riding from leg-yield to half-pass on the same rein. When changing position from right to left, or from left to right, allow three steps on a straight line to allow time for a half-halt to rebalance the horse and to reposition him. The amount of flexion and bend should be the same in each direction.

Leg-yield

Leg-yield is 'inside leg to outside hand'

Once you can keep your horse straight, i.e. positioned to the right or to the left, all that is required to ride a leg-yield is to allow the horse to move sideways by softening your outside rein a little, and using slightly more inside leg. When you want to stop the leg-yield, firm up your outside rein and use less inside leg. To ask for more bend in the ribs in the leg-yield, ride it as shoulder-fore on the diagonal.

The aids for leg yield are:
- Prepare your horse for leg-yield by positioning him to the right or left with your inside leg keeping him into your outside rein.
- Increase the angle and bend slightly so that the horse is in shoulder-out. This can be done on a circle, around a corner, or on a straight line.
- To go into leg-yield, the horse must step forwards and sideways away from the direction in which his nose is pointing.
- The horse steps from your inside leg to your outside hand.

The asking aids are:
- Apply pressure with the inside leg (at the girth) in the form of nudges with the calf to activate the inside hind leg.
- The outside rein controls the position of the neck and shoulders.

The supporting aids are:
- The inside rein maintains flexion so that the horse is facing away from the direction in which he is being asked to go.
- Use the outside thigh pressure (leg behind the girth) to support the ribcage.

Half-pass

Half pass is 'outside leg to inside hand'

Half-pass should never be presented as just the haunches swinging to one side to avoid taking weight. It is important that the angle of the half-pass and the positioning of the horse is correctly executed so that the hind legs are taking weight (evenly loaded) and can work with *Schubkraft* (pushing power). The forehand must lighten for the horse to move forwards and sideways with ease.

The more of an angle at which the horse is ridden, i.e. the more the forehand is allowed to lead, the easier the half-pass is. When riding half-pass with a novice horse, therefore, the forehand should be allowed to lead more. This position is as for a shoulder-fore. With an advanced horse, the horse's forehand and haunches should be in alignment, i.e. the horse is straighter (in position).

The aids for half-pass are:
- Prepare your horse for the half-pass by positioning him to the right or left with your inside leg keeping him into your outside rein.
- Increase the angle and bend slightly so that the horse is in shoulder-fore. This can be done on a circle, around a corner, or on a straight line.
- To go into half-pass, the horse must step forwards and sideways in the direction in which his nose is pointing.
- The horse steps from your outside leg to your inside hand.

The asking aids are:
- Apply pressure with the outside leg (behind the girth) in the form of nudges with the calf to activate the outside hind leg.
- Use thigh pressure to move the ribcage over.
- Maintain the position of the horse's head with the inside rein with his forehead facing the direction in which he is being asked to go.

The supporting aids are:
- The inside lower leg acts at the girth to maintain rhythm and forwardness.
- The inside thigh supports the ribcage.
- The outside rein softens to allow the forehand to lead the movement.

TRAINING TIPS
- Use half-halts to lighten the forehand to make going sideways easier. These have to be applied before, during and after the movement. A horse that is on his forehand will allow his hind legs to escape and trail them along behind.

- A well-trained horse will travel forwards and sideways with ease. Once he is set up for the half-pass or the leg-yield he should keep going of his own accord without having to be reminded en route!
- Make sure the horse works on three tracks in all lateral movements. Then you can be sure the hind legs are evenly taking weight. A very supple horse is able to work on four tracks, but this must be carefully monitored to make sure the hind legs do not escape to the outside and lose engagement.

PROBLEM SOLVING

- If the horse has a weak right hind, he will move his haunches all too willingly to the right in a half-pass right to avoid taking weight on his right hind. He will find half-pass to the left more difficult as the right hind has to swing across under his body. Riding along the diagonal of the school, changing the bend from leg-yield to half-pass and back again is a very good exercise for strengthening a weak hind leg.
- Riding renvers (haunches-out) along the track or on circles is a good way to strengthen the hind legs and to loosen the horse's hips so that he can take bigger sideways steps. This in turn improves straightness and impulsion in lateral work, and particularly when ridden forwards on straight lines.
- Use shoulder-fore and shoulder-in as warm-up exercises for half-pass. A horse must be able to do shoulder-in before progressing to half-pass.

Exercise 5 (jumping)
Accuracy when placing the horse on the approach
AIM
The aim of this exercise is to use challenging obstacles so that the rider has to line the horse up with the centre of the jump for the best approach.

THE EXERCISE
Set out three obstacles around the arena as in Diagram 29 so that they can be approached on a straight line. They should be built at a height of about 1m (3ft), though start with the fences at 0.5m (1ft 6in) as a warm-up.

The first fence (a) is an upright with cones on the ground on the approach and on the landing to mark out the take-off zone and landing zone. The rider should aim to keep the horse straight between both sets of cones, before take-off and after landing. The second fence (b) is an arrowhead to be jumped over the apex of the arrow, the angle of which should be 90 degrees, and the third fence (c) is built as a parallel, but with the top poles crossed over nearer one wing than the other. The narrowest place to jump the fence is where the poles cross. The rider has the choice whether to jump the narrowest point or the centre of the jump. These fences can be approached from walk, trot or canter.

WHAT TO LOOK FOR

Each fence should be ridden as an individual fence to start with, making sure that your technique is correct before linking the fences together in a mini course. Practise approaching from trot first to make sure that your line of approach to each individual fence is accurate and to familiarize the horse with the different fences. It is harder for a horse to put in a refusal from trot than it is from canter. In trot, the forelegs lift off the ground one after

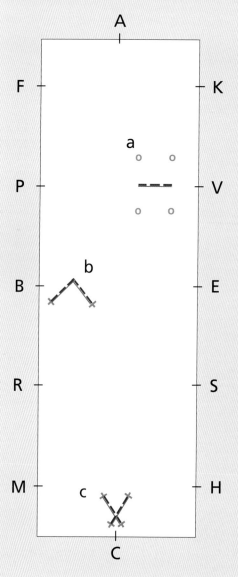

Diagram 29 *Exercise 5 Challenging obstacles such as uprights with marker cones, arrowheads and off-centre cross poles, for practice in bringing a horse in to a jump straight for the best approach.*

the other making it difficult for the horse to plant himself in front of a fence. In canter both forelegs push off the ground together which, therefore, makes it easier for the horse to refuse.

Line the horse up on approach to the mid-point of each fence. Begin with the upright (a); this is the easiest jump to approach straight as cones have been placed to guide you. The line of approach to the arrowhead (b) should be straight into the narrowest part of the jump. With the parallel (c), line up with either the narrowest point or the middle of the fence but stick to your chosen line of approach and do not be tempted to waver. All the fences can, in theory, be jumped from both directions, but jumping an arrowhead from the pointed side takes a great deal of accuracy!

TRAINING TIPS
- Warm-up exercises such as stretching on a long rein in all three gaits and transitions, especially walk-canter-walk transitions to put the horse's weight more on his hocks, are invaluable preparation for any jumping exercise.
- Circles of different sizes will loosen the horse and make sure he is working into the outside rein before attempting to jump. Although the approach to each fence is straight, you must have the horse working into the outside aids in between the obstacles to make sure the canter is balanced. Have a plan for what to do after landing: look ahead and plan the next approach, or rebalance the horse with lateral movements such as shoulder-in or half-pass.
- You need to make sure that your horse is obedient to your aids and that the brakes work, so that you can ask for half-halts or halt transitions at any time.

PROBLEM SOLVING
- The horse should approach each fence willingly and confidently but should be under control. There is a difference between the horse **taking** the rider into the fence and the horse **tanking** into a fence! In the former, the rider should always have the ability to stop the horse,

even if only a stride or two away from the fence without taking emergency measures to swerve away from the line of approach. (**Note** Asking the horse to stop before a fence and then proceeding to jump does not teach the horse to refuse. Quite the opposite is actually true. It just re-affirms the rider's aids and makes sure that the horse is balanced before jumping.) If the horse has trust in the rider, he believes what he is being asked to do. The horse should wait for the command to continue forwards to the fence. If the horse is tanking, the rider has no control over the speed at which the horse approaches the fence; there will be no brakes and stopping will not be possible. A good training exercise is to canter towards the fence, walk or halt three or four strides away, then canter, trot, or walk to the take-off point. A well-balanced horse should be able to jump from walk!

- If you are not straight yourself, then your horse will jump to one side and you will find it very difficult to stay on course. The arrowhead fence will be particularly difficult, and you may find that you jump to the side of the actual point of the fence. Lower the fences, and practise your lines of approach until they are accurate before raising the fences again. Grid work, or cavalletti, is a good exercise to do to improve straightness.

- If your horse rushes after the fences, make a downwards transition to trot, walk or halt after each fence, but keep the horse straight when you do so to ensure he brings both hind legs under him and remains working into an even contact. Try to make the transition within four steps of landing and avoid letting him swerve to one side. He must respond quickly to your aids after each fence. If you are not disciplined enough to ask for the transition on a straight line, after a few attempts at the jumps your horse will most likely be on his forehand and leaning against the contact, making it hard to stop him. A balanced horse is a responsive horse. There is no fun in jumping fences on an unbalanced horse who is out of control!

Exercise 6 (jumping)
Jumps on a serpentine

AIM
The aim of this exercise is to improve accuracy to the centre of obstacles when coming off a turn or curved line of approach.

THE EXERCISE
Set out three obstacles on the centre line of the school as shown in Diagram 30. The outer two can be upright fences, and the centre fence a parallel. It is useful if each fence can be jumped from both directions. They can be from 0.5m (1ft 6in) to 1.m (3ft) in height. The parallel should be the same width as it is high. Place each fence so that it can be jumped on a three-loop serpentine. The fences can be ridden from trot or canter.

WHAT TO LOOK FOR
Begin on the right rein around the school. Aim for three straight steps with each fence: one before the fence (the approach), one over it and one after the fence (the landing). Ride in trot towards the first upright (a) on the right rein

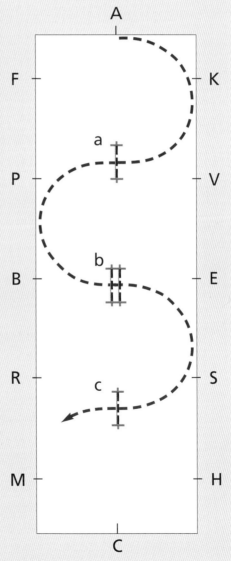

Diagram 30 *Exercise 6 Jumps on the centre line of the school to be jumped on a serpentine. The line of the approach must be accurate and the horse straight.*

(right position). After the third straight step, position the horse to the left and ride a curved line to the left, following the route of the three-loop serpentine. Take the parallel in the middle (b) straight, change to right position and jump the second upright (c) from the right rein, straightening on the approach to the fence. This exercise requires changes of flexion and bend (position) before and after each fence, though the horse must be straight to actually jump the fence.

When riding this exercise in canter, the canter must be collected enough (see Collection, page 174) for the horse to bend-straighten-bend over the fence. It helps if the horse offers a flying change over the fence but this will only happen of the horse is balanced. The horse may, however, change legs behind out of self-preservation if the rider is leaning to the inside in anticipation of the forthcoming loop. If the horse does not change legs over the fence, or changes behind and becomes disunited, then you must bring the horse back to trot or walk, and ask for the correct canter lead directly after the fence. As with the previous exercise, the horse must be sufficiently on your aids for you to make a transition and correct the canter lead before changing direction onto the next loop of the serpentine.

TRAINING TIPS

- Warm up first with the fence poles on the ground and familiarise the horse with the serpentine in walk and trot on a long rein so that he stretches and loosens up.
- This exercise can be ridden with a cavalletti instead of each fence for practising changing leg in canter either in the air or after each fence. (See Exercise 1 on page 153 for riding flying changes)
- This exercise can also be ridden approaching the fences on an angle. When jumping fences on an angle, the line of approach must still be straight along the line the rider has chosen to place the horse. For example, when approaching a fence at a 45 degree angle, the horse must be straight through his body so that he can take off from both hind feet, jump with his neck in line with his spine, and stretch his neck forwards in line with his chest. The rider should still line the horse up on approach to the centre of the obstacle. (See Figure 5.8)

Figure 5.8 *Jo and Trevor jump this upright fence from a straight take-off, preparing to turn after the fence.*

PROBLEM SOLVING

- If the horse falls in around the loops, he will not be balanced for the fences, and may refuse or run out. Make sure you have sufficient inside leg on to give the horse support and to keep him working into your outside rein.
- If the horse drifts out around the loops of the serpentine, you should make sure he is working into your outside aids in position so that you can keep him straight on curved lines (hind feet stepping into the tracks of the forefeet).
- If the horse rushes away around the loops, then add a 10m circle in each loop to help him to calm down and relax before continuing to the next fence.

6 Collection (*Versammlung*)

Versammlung is the German word for scale 6, Collection, in the scales of training, its literal translation being 'the act of putting together' or 'assembling'. This assembly is really the culmination of building the horse as a whole using the scales of training as stages in the building process until the final aim of him working through his back, true suppleness, or *Durchlässigkeit* is achieved. Collection is the final scale of training or the ability of the horse to take weight behind and to work with the poll as the highest point.

The Degrees and Applications of Collection

Collection develops in degrees according to the standard the horse has reached. The early stage of collection is balance, when the novice horse is able to carry a rider on his back without leaning on the reins for support. This can be described as the 'baby stage' of collection, as the horse has to learn to take weight behind in order to balance with a rider on board. A horse who is not in balance takes his weight on his forehand and leans on the reins for support, which takes us back to Contact, the fourth scale of training.

You should not be able to hear the footsteps of a balanced and collected horse. A balanced horse moves quietly over the ground and does not disturb the surface of the arena. A horse who is on his forehand and unbalanced, with no degree of collection, will thunder along kicking up clouds of dust as he goes!

If a horse is working in collection he is said to be working in an uphill outline. This uphill appearance is a result of the haunches lowering, rather than the forehand lifting. As the haunches take weight, the forehand becomes lighter making the horse more manoeuvrable and able to perform advanced movements such as piaffe and canter pirouettes.

Collection is a culmination of the other scales.

- Collected gaits cover less ground per stride than working gaits. The steps must be **rhythmic**. (See Rhythm, page 21)
- A horse cannot collect if he is stiff. He must be relaxed in order for him to be

supple – *Losgelassen* –enough to tuck his pelvis and take weight behind. (See Suppleness, page 61)

- The horse must work into a soft **contact** in order to collect. Working in balance without leaning on the reins is achieved with half-halts and transitions. (See Contact, page 86)
- What the steps lose in length they must gain in height otherwise the steps are flat and lacking **impulsion**. (See Impulsion, page 117) The steps should have a springiness to them, which is known as cadence.
- A horse cannot collect if he is crooked; he must be **straight**. (See Straightness, page 147)

Without balance, the first degree of collection, the horse is unable to work in a rhythm; we therefore come full circle back to the first scale. As the horse progresses in his training over many years, each scale is revisited and improved upon along the way.

(See Figures 6.1a, b and c)

Figures 6.1a, b and c *Degrees of collection. All the horses are working as actively behind as they are in front. The neck position changes as the horse becomes more able to 'sit' behind. a) (above left) Archie showing good balance for a novice horse after only a few weeks of training, in a relaxed outline with his nose correctly just in front of the vertical. b) (above right) Norman at elementary level showing a good degree of engagement. His forehand is raised correctly and he is going forwards confidently. c) (right) Amadeus at Grand Prix level showing a light, elegant collected trot with good joint flexion and a correct neck position with his poll the highest point. He is looking for something to spook at and is a bit distracted!*

Collection in jumping

In order to learn how to jump, a horse must firstly be in balance in all three gaits. (See Figure 6.2) At a later stage in his training, a horse who is truly able to collect will knock the spots off the opposition in a jump-off against the clock because he will be able to turn very neatly between the obstacles and to have enough impulsion to clear high jumps from a short approach. He will be able to alter his bascule (shape over the fence) according to the type of obstacle, in order to be efficient with his impulsion, saving it for tight turns and launching himself over bigger and wider fences. His forehand will be light and he will be athletic, reducing wear and tear on his joints.

Figure 6.2 *In order to learn how to jump, a young horse must firstly be balanced in all three gaits, taking weight behind. Norman in a lovely uphill canter.*

Collection in dressage

In dressage, collected work culminates in advanced movements such as piaffe, passage, canter pirouettes (also useful for the show-jumper to master) and tempi changes. These all require plenty of lift through the forehand, which is the result of the horse being able to 'sit' on his haunches. Only a fit horse with well-developed musculature will be able to work properly at the higher levels. Many horses can work well up to the level of four- and three-time changes in canter, and half canter pirouettes, but far fewer reach the pinnacle of the Grand Prix in dressage and Grade A in showjumping. Horses who reach the top and can sustain their achievement over time are the ones who have been properly trained. There are many who are one-hit wonders and this is often due to injuries occurring because the scales of training were not adhered to. Short cuts in the early days of a horse's training will inevitably shorten his career.

There is no extension without collection

Without collection, a horse cannot extend properly. A passage is a collected version of an extended trot, maintaining the same pushing power of the haunches and desire to go forwards. A horse who can execute a correct piaffe with a light contact and lowered haunches is able to remain perfectly balanced and can be asked to go into medium trot directly from piaffe. A horse who can collect sufficiently to do a neat canter pirouette remains light and 'off the ground' enough to do one-time tempi changes with ease. Many riders struggle with medium trot at the lower levels of dressage and fruitlessly hurry the horse around the school in an effort to lengthen the stride, adamant that he must go forwards at all costs. But this just results in a horse rushing along on his forehand with short, tense steps and the hind legs paddling along behind, not taking weight at all. If these riders spent time teaching a horse to collect, he would be able to do medium trot steps with ease.

 ## How a Horse Collects

Collection begins at the back end of the horse with his pelvis tucking under from the croup, his back lifting and his abdominal muscles tightening, which supports the back from underneath and also acts to draw the hind legs forwards under the haunches. The hind legs begin at the lumbo-sacral joint (point of croup) and if a horse is unable to coil his loins from this point, he will not be able to flex his stifle or hock joints, as all these joints work together. If the pelvis cannot tuck under, the back legs cannot flex and come under the haunches, therefore they cannot take weight, and the horse cannot be balanced. He can certainly not work in collection.

As a result of the horse tucking his pelvis and raising his back, his neck arches from the withers and reaches forward into the rein contact like a telescope. The nuchal ligament supports the horse's spine along its length and splays out to connect the withers and crest to the neck vertebrae. The top and middle neck muscles appear long and smooth along the length of the neck between the head and the shoulder. The muscle underneath the neck will be relaxed.

A horse who is able to lift his forehand will become wider in his chest, as the pectoral muscles between the front legs become stronger and more able to support the forehand from underneath. These muscles increase in size particularly with lateral work. A horse should reach forward to the bit with a relaxed poll and jaw once his posture and balance is correct.

It is incorrect for the hind legs to step so far forward under the belly that they no longer carry weight. This can result from forcing the horse to work with his hind legs under before the rest of his body is able to conform. This horse can lower his back end without coiling his loins because his hind legs have disappeared in a frontward direction and are avoiding carrying weight. Because the lumbo-sacral joint is not flexed, neither are the stifles or hocks. These straight stiff legs reach too far forward under the belly and the horse looks as though he will fall back on his tail. Often the front legs come behind the shoulders, avoiding supporting the forehand, giving the impression that this horse's front and back feet are hobbled together. This is typical of horses who are forced to piaffe before they are ready. They appear rounded, but the neck will be dropped from the withers, the nose comes behind the vertical and the feet shuffle along. Poll problems are common in horses with this false roundness. Such horses will need to be retrained from the beginning.

 ## The Rider's Influence on Collection

In order to collect, the horse must be responsive to light aids from the rider. This takes time to establish, and must be started from the beginning of the horse's training and not left until the next dressage test requires a collected trot! Horses have to be *taught* to be light to the aids but this must be done in the right way and never forcefully. Some horses are more sensitive than others, so you must bear the individual in mind when training. A firm aid to one horse is far too insignificant to another and will be ignored. A young unbalanced horse needs much more support from the rider's position, and clear obvious aids but this does not mean rough aids.

Collection has nothing to do with holding the head and neck of the horse forcefully in position and kicking to get him to go forward into a short, tight rein contact. The horse will not want to go forward and become 'stuffy' or difficult. He cannot possibly move willingly from the rider's aids with tense disconnected hind legs and stiff joints. If the poll and jaw are not relaxed, the horse will not yield or soften to the rein contact, he will not lift his back, and he will not engage his hind legs.

Some riders try to raise the poll with the hands alone and hold the horse's head on the bit without any regard for the rest of the horse. The underneath muscle of the neck will bulge, and the horse will appear to have a dip in front of his withers. His poll will be tight and he will lean against the bit with a locked jaw. He will hollow his back and trail his hind legs with saggy, beer-belly

Figure 6.3 *The test of collection is: can the horse stretch forwards and downwards correctly? Whatever level of training the horse achieves, he should always be able to stretch. Jo and Trevor showing correct stretching forwards and downwards.*

abdominal muscles. His hind legs will be stiff and push the horse along without taking any weight at all, requiring the horse to carry himself on his front legs with his weight taken on his forehand. He may become crooked and push his haunches to one side to avoid the discomfort in his back.

Quite often these horses are ridden or lunged in draw reins to lower the neck. The neck may lower but the back remains tense and the hind legs disengaged. Simply forcing the neck to be round does not help the horse to use his back and certainly does not collect him in any way, shape or form. Once the draw reins are taken off, the horse will lift his neck even higher as the muscles he has been using to fight the reins will have become stronger, and so he becomes even more upside down than before. The only way to help this situation is to go back to the first two scales of training, Rhythm and Suppleness, concentrating on correct stretching through the back (see Suppleness, page 61). (See Figure 6.3)

Once the horse is balanced under the rider (taking weight behind) then the rider's aids become more fine-tuned. To collect the horse, you need to ride many half-halts (see Contact, page 96 and Figures 6.4a and b) and perfect the halt and transitions. Rein-back is another useful collecting exercise which teaches the horse to tuck his pelvis under.

Movements that influence collection
Halt
The most important collecting movement to perfect is the halt. In halt, the horse should stand still with all four legs square. He should be on the bit with his nose vertical or slightly in front of the vertical, but not against the rein contact.

In a good halt, no aids should be necessary to maintain the halt once the horse has stood still. You must be able to keep your horse straight in order to ride a correct halt, and to ensure he *is* straight bring him into the halt by preparing him with half-halts to ask him to step under with the hind legs, i.e. '1,2,3 stop', rather than jamming on the brakes suddenly.

Figures 6.4a and b
a) (far left) The way to collect the horse is to half-halt correctly, bracing the back and closing the legs to bring the hind legs under the body and to lift the horse's back. b) (left) When bracing the back, the small of the rider's back is pressed forwards slightly, to hold the hips in an upright position without coming onto the fork, and upwards towards the breastbone. The rider must remain sitting level in the saddle. At the same time, the rider must close the thighs, knees and calves to lift the horse's middle, enabling him to step under behind, and to press him forwards to the bit, so that he arches his neck forwards to the bit. In both these photos, you can clearly see the riders pressing the small of their backs forwards. The Germans say 'Kreuz anziehen', i.e. 'press the back', to describe this action. The riders' hands remain still, without pulling back.

The aids for halt, are to sit up tall, firm up the back and stomach muscles, pressing your lower back forwards and upwards towards your breastbone (bracing the back, or in German: *Kreuz anziehen*) close the legs, and stop moving. When you are motionless, i.e. maintaining your postural strength and sitting still but not giving any actual aids, your horse will stop. Your legs and back close the hind legs under the horse so that he stops in an uphill position rather than downhill (on his forehand). The contact should remain constant, and not become stronger than the body aids. If this is the case, you are pulling. Keep your elbows in place against your sides and avoid clenching your fingers. Pressing your thumb down on the rein against the first finger should be sufficient to prevent the reins slipping through your hands. The other fingers should be gently closed in a fist. Once the horse has stopped, the reins should soften to allow him to remain in balance, or self-carriage. Soften your body aids slightly to allow him to stand still in balance; to reiterate, give no aids, but just keep your position.

A halt has a transition into and out of it and in the same way as any other transition, therefore, the halt should have impulsion. The horse has to be collected in the halt in order to stand without moving but is, in effect, standing to attention ready and willing to proceed into the next movement as soon as you request it. A test of collection is that a horse should be able to halt at any moment from any gait, on request. He should also be able to go forwards into any gait from the halt.

Figures 6.5a, b and c *a)* (above left) *Amadeus in halt; note how much more this advanced horse is under behind in the halt than the horses in the following photographs. b)* (above centre) *It is important for the young horse to stand still in the halt; you get marked for 'immobility' in a dressage test, and so it is important to establish this! Heinrich, a novice horse, is standing still but the halt is not quite square behind. c)* (above right) *Trevor in halt on his own in the field. Trevor competes in affiliated show jumping and is also a medium-level horse. A horse who is fit and well and working correctly should stand with his hind legs under his body with ease – even without a rider!*

For example, the horse should be able to halt directly from the medium canter and, conversely, go into passage from the halt if he is truly collected, though this takes many years of training to achieve. At novice level it is an achievement to halt from the working trot! (See Figures 6.5a, b and c)

Transitions

A **transition** is a change of gait, i.e. from walk to trot, walk to halt and so on. A **direct transition** is where you miss a gait, i.e. go from walk to canter, trot to halt etc. A **transition within the gait** means going from working trot to medium trot, collected walk to extended walk etc.

To ride good transitions, make sure your aids are clear. Prepare for each transition well, making sure that your horse is softly on the bit so that he benefits from using his back and hindquarters correctly. He should be going forward enough to have impulsion to take him into the next gait, whether you are riding an upward or downward transition, but without rushing against your hands. You both need to be in good balance, i.e. you should be able to soften your reins without everything falling to pieces! Check that your own position is good enough for you to have effective use of your legs and upper body, maintaining an elastic contact.

Prepare each transition by keeping your horse straight and balanced, and ask him to take his weight on his hocks by using half-halts. You need to feel that he is lifting his back underneath you in order for the transition to be clear and precise.

Rein-back

Rein-back is a very effective exercise to teach a horse how to tuck his pelvis and to take weight behind. In the rein-back the horse steps backwards in a rounded outline with his back raised and his haunches under. The legs move in diagonal pairs. The steps should be regular and in a two-time rhythm. He should pick up his feet clearly and not scuff his toes along the ground.

Rein-back, when ridden correctly, improves the engagement of the hind legs, and teaches the horse to tuck his haunches further under, so that it looks as though his back end is lower than the front. As he steps backwards, his neck outline should remain the same but this is only possible if his hind legs are lined up with his front legs, i.e. the horse is straight.

AIDS FOR REIN-BACK

To ride a correct rein-back, firstly halt square with good balance. Take both legs behind the girth by stretching your thighs down and back and nudge with both calves simultaneously to ask the horse to move his hind legs under his body. To ask him to go backwards, ease your weight forwards towards your crotch, so that you feel as though you are sitting closer to the pommel of the saddle. This will lighten the back of your seat and, in effect, 'open the back door' to allow the horse to raise his loins and tuck his pelvis under. Ease your shoulders about a couple of centimetres forward, which will make you feel as though your weight is forward over your knees.

Maintain a steady contact on the reins. The rein pressure increases slightly as you ask the horse to move with both calves. As he steps into the resisting (but not pulling) reins, he then becomes aware that you are sitting differently from normal. In this position with your weight slightly forward, he feels that the back of your seat is lighter, which tells him it is easier to go backwards than forwards. Keep your knees and front of the thighs close to the saddle to 'close the front door' so that he only has the option to go backwards.

As he takes his first step back, immediately soften the contact to reward him. This has the effect of allowing him to arch his neck forwards to the bit in order to balance as the haunches tuck under and his back lifts. He should stay softly in your

Figure 6.6 *In the rein-back a horse should tuck his pelvis under and take weight behind. It is a very useful exercise for teaching horses how to tuck. Amadeus shows a good lowering of the haunches in this rein-back though he could be more relaxed and yielding more to the contact.*

reins so try not to drop the contact altogether. Keep your position for three or four steps backward. Then sit up straight on your seat bones, bring your legs forward into their normal position again, and halt. Reward the horse with a pat or verbal praise. Then walk forwards again. (See Figure 6.6)

Movements that require extreme collection
Piaffe

The FEI definition of piaffe is: 'The piaffe is a highly collected, cadenced, elevated diagonal movement giving the impression of being in place. The horse's back is supple and elastic. The quarters are slightly lowered, the haunches with active hocks are well engaged giving great freedom, lightness and mobility to the shoulders and forehand. Each diagonal pair of feet is raised and returned to the ground alternately, with an even cadence.'

AIDS FOR PIAFFE

To go from extra-collected trot or walk into piaffe, brace your back enough to hold the horse on the spot more, inhibiting forward motion. He should be allowed to creep forwards as he steps into piaffe to keep him thinking forwards. What you do *not* want him to do is to use the excuse of the forehand lifting to rear up! If he does attempt to rear up, give him a very firm nudge in the ribs to ask him in no uncertain terms to go forwards. You must have your wits about you and react promptly. Remain in an upright position in the saddle, and maintain a consistent contact with the reins. When a horse rears, many riders lean forwards and give the reins, which just rewards the horse for rearing. It is far better to ride the horse forwards before he actually stands up. To rear, the hind legs need to be 'on the spot'. By making sure the hind legs step forwards, the rear should be avoided. If the horse is not in front of your aids at all times he may run backwards.

Your hips should mirror the motion of the horse's back exactly, which is a very slight ripple of the back muscles. Avoid pushing and shoving with your seat, as this will prevent the horse's loins from lifting, and his hind legs will not step under behind.

Press down on the stirrups to brace the calves, and use them near the girth. If you bring your lower legs back too far, the horse may mistake your aids for those for rein-back. Use the calves together to keep the hind legs moving in trot rhythm. The thighs should remain soft as, more than the thighs, it should be your back and stomach muscles that are holding the horse.

Do not allow the horse to take a strong contact otherwise the activity of the hind legs will be lost. Use half-halts frequently to keep the horse balanced and with his poll the highest point. Keep a soft contact. If the piaffe is truly balanced, you should be able to loosen the reins completely.

Piaffe is a very collected movement, which is performed on the spot, with the legs moving in diagonal pairs as with the trot. It develops from a horse being strong enough in his back to take a greater proportion of his weight on his haunches than on his forehand. In a correct piaffe the horse should lower his haunches, tucking his pelvis under, giving the impression that he could sit on the ground. The forehand lifts with a well-arched neck, the poll being the highest point. This is only achievable with a correctly trained and well-balanced horse. The steps must be rhythmical for piaffe to be correctly executed. (See Figure 6.7)

Figure 6.7 Piaffe develops from the horse being strong enough in his back to take a greater proportion of his weight on his haunches. This rider is sitting in a lovely upright position and is able to maintain the piaffe while releasing the rein contact – a good test of balance.

Passage

The FEI definition of passage is: 'A measured, very collected, very elevated and very cadenced trot. It is characterized by a pronounced engagement of the quarters, a more accentuated flexion of the knees and hocks and the graceful elasticity of the movement. Each diagonal pair of feet is raised and returned to the ground alternately with cadence and has a prolonged phase of support compared to the phase of suspension.'

AIDS FOR PASSAGE

Passage, like piaffe, can be developed from the extra-collected trot. In trot sit upright, draw both legs back slightly and hold the horse's middle with your thighs. Brace your back to hold the trot steps, but think of lifting the steps off the ground with your thighs and back to develop springiness, or cadence. Your back must be supple enough to accommodate the bounce in the period of suspension from diagonal pair to diagonal pair. Your lower legs maintain the rhythm and the forwardness. Allow the forward motion with soft reins. If the reins are too strong, you will inhibit the pushing power (*Schubkraft*) of the hind legs.

Passage can also be developed from medium trot. Shorten the medium trot steps by bracing your back (half-halts) and the horse's middle with your thighs. Your legs should be slightly behind the girth, asking the horse to push off from the ground with each stride. What the steps lose in length, they should gain in height. This method is a very effective way of maintaining impulsion and the desire to go forwards. Make frequent transitions from medium trot to passage, and from passage to medium trot.

Passage is an extremely collected trot with a lot of elevation. The best way I can describe it is as a collected version of a medium trot. The horse has to be strong enough to spring off the ground at each step, travelling forward as he does so. He should maintain self-carriage and outline with good articulation of his leg joints. All four legs should come off the ground to the same height and the two-beat trot rhythm must remain regular. (See Figure 6.8)

Figure 6.8 *In passage, a horse must maintain the trot rhythm and spring off the ground with a huge amount of elevation, and cadence. Amadeus gives it his all!*

 ## Exercises to Improve Collection

Exercise 1 (dressage and jumping)
Using ground poles at walk distance
AIM
To use rein-back, transitions and direct transitions for developing collected gaits.

THE EXERCISE

Place up to eight ground poles at walking distance, 0.8m (2ft 6in) apart on the short side at the A end of the school. Starting on the left rein, walk over the poles with your horse on the bit. Maintain the energy in the walk steps after the poles, and make a transition to collected trot directly after the poles. Ride a halt transition directly from trot at R. From the halt, proceed directly into collected canter. At S, ride a transition to halt, rein-back a few steps and halt again. Ride a transition into collected trot and another into collected walk just before the poles. Start the exercise again; it can be repeated three or four times before changing the rein and riding the same pattern of transitions on the right rein. (See Diagram 31)

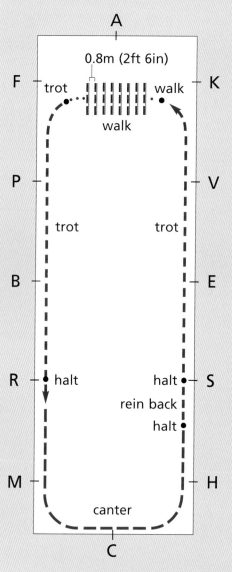

WHAT TO LOOK FOR

Make sure you loosen the horse on a long rein in walk, trot and canter before starting the exercise. The horse should be ready to walk over the poles on the bit from the beginning, but after the exercise you can loosen him up and relax him by walking over the poles on a long rein allowing him to stretch forwards and downwards. The transitions should be accurate, and

Diagram 31 Exercise 1 Poles placed at walk distance apart on the short side of the school. The exercise includes work with transitions, direct transitions and rein-back.

the horse prepared for each one with half-halts. Keep him straight to help him engage both hind legs under his body. When riding the halt-to-canter transition, make sure the halt has sufficient energy (impulsion) for the horse to spring forwards and upwards into canter with a light forehand.

TRAINING TIPS

- The aids for the rein-back are on page 182 but firstly have a square halt with impulsion, so that the horse is prepared for whatever you ask for next. If he halts with no energy and is half asleep, you stand no chance of getting him to move forwards or backwards! The horse must want to go *forwards* before you can ask him to go backwards.

- When cantering directly from a rein-back, the canter aid should be applied once the horse has gone backwards the required number of steps.

- The number of steps in a rein-back depends on the ability of the horse. One horse's length is about three to four steps, and this is a good number of steps to start with. Only riding one or two steps does not give a horse the chance to relax through his back and establish stepping backwards in diagonal pairs. You should feel for the horse relaxing through his back. If the horse is tense and raises his head, hollowing his back, he should be ridden forwards again and prepared better in the halt.

- When approaching the poles after the trot, try to make the walk transition as close to the poles as possible to help the horse step under behind. Having a definite place to walk (i.e. just before the first pole) makes you focus more on preparing the horse. Be careful, though, that you do not make some sort of emergency stop by pulling at the reins!

PROBLEM SOLVING

There are many things that can go wrong in a transition, hence the list below!

- Excessive rein aids in a downward transition can cause a horse to overbend as he tries to dodge the pressure on his mouth. Pulling on the reins causes him to run forwards against the contact and grind to a stop on the forehand.

- Not keeping the legs on or using uneven leg pressure in the rein-back can cause a horse to drift one way or the other. If you are not sitting straight, the horse will not halt straight or remain straight in the rein-back.
- If the reins are too loose, the horse will not remain on the bit and not learn how to yield to the rein contact through his poll and jaw.
- If you do not soften the reins once the horse has halted, he might step backwards and assume you want a rein-back. If you collapse around the middle once your horse has halted, he may move because you are not sitting still enough.
- When riding a half-halt, using the reins alone, or even just the outside rein, does not tell the horse to step under with his hind legs. A half-halt has to be a coordination of seat, leg and reins, not just the reins. Taking your legs off in a half-halt or a downward transition allows the hind legs to trail behind, while sitting back in the saddle causes the horse to hollow his back and go against the rein.
- A correct position in the saddle must be maintained. Sitting back in the saddle in a transition causes the horse to hollow his back and push his hind legs away behind. This fault is often accompanied by a rider pushing their legs forwards and ramming their heels down and forwards instead of closing the legs against the horse's sides. Sticking your legs forwards in this way is like stepping on the gas pedal and your horse may shoot forwards. You will then have to resort to pulling like mad on the reins to stop him!

Exercise 2 (dressage and jumping)
Circles and half-circles with shoulder-in and travers
AIM
The aim of this exercise is to collect the horse by improving the engagement of the hind legs and the lightness of the forehand using lateral movements. Lateral movements develop from correct bending on circles and turns.

THE EXERCISE

Loosen the horse first on a long rein in walk, trot and canter. Starting at the corner before F on the left rein, ride a volte. From the volte, ride directly into shoulder-in left maintaining the engagement of the inside hind leg, which should have been established on the volte. From B to E change the rein, riding a half 10m circle left to X, and a half 10m circle right to E. At the track, proceed in shoulder-in right to H and ride a volte in the corner to the right directly from shoulder-in. From the volte ride travers across the short side into a second volte to the right in the corner before changing the rein across the diagonal in medium trot. After the diagonal at K ride a volte in the corner to the left, followed by travers left across the short side. You have now returned to the first volte to the left ready to repeat the exercise again. Ride the exercise three or four times on each rein. It can be ridden in walk, trot and canter. (See Diagram 32)

WHAT TO LOOK FOR

The voltes and half-circles give you the chance to make sure a horse is bending properly, and that you maintain forwardness. If the lateral steps in shoulder-in and travers are

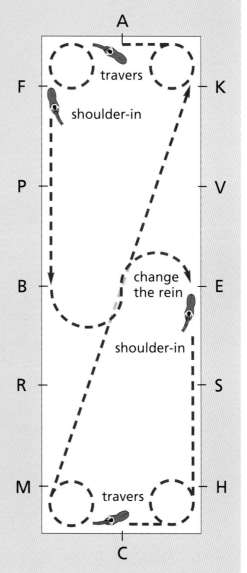

Diagram 32 Exercise 2 Riding small circles with shoulder-in and travers improves collection by engaging the hind legs and lightening the forehand.

balanced, and collected, you should be able to soften the inside rein at any time. (See Chapters 2 and 4 for the aids for shoulder-in and travers respectively)

Make sure the change of bend at X, from one half-circle to the other, is straight. Use this opportunity to ride a half-halt or a downward transition to help engagement of the haunches. If your lateral work is good, then this transition will be easy. If your lateral work is poor, then the transition will be a mess!

Once the horse is supple and collected on both reins, the objective has been achieved, so finish the exercise.

TRAINING TIPS

- The circle is the basis of all lateral movements and it is most important it is accurate. It must start and finish at the same point and be a geometrically round shape. A horse must bend through his whole body to achieve an accurate circle. His head should be in line with the middle of his chest and his hind feet should step in the tracks of his forefeet, i.e. he must be straight.
- A volte is a small circle, 6–8m in diameter, and should have all the same qualities as a circle.
- Remember to stretch the horse frequently to maintain relaxation and looseness.
- Half-halt before every change of movement to balance the horse and to make sure he is taking weight behind.
- When changing leg through canter over X, this can be ridden through trot, walk, halt, or as a flying change.

PROBLEM SOLVING

- A horse should be able to bend equally in both directions. If he finds the exercise easier one way than the other, do not make the mistake of riding the worst rein more often. Just continue to improve the horse on both reins. If he understands the exercise on the easier rein, this should help him to get the hang of it on his more difficult rein.
- If the horse is not so supple and finds 6m voltes too small, he may swing his haunches out, in which case you should work on 10m circles.

- If he becomes tense and hurries the lateral work, repeat the voltes or small circles two or three times each to re-establish the rhythm of the gait.

Exercise 3 (dressage)
Pirouettes in walk and canter
AIM
The aim of this exercise is to increase the strength and carrying ability of the haunches and lightness of the forehand, improving collection. Basically, when riding demi- and full pirouettes, the front end turns around the back end, with the hind legs taking enough weight for the horse to turn his forehand with ease.

HOW TO RIDE A DEMI-PIROUETTE IN WALK AND CANTER
The aids for riding a demi-pirouette in walk and canter are given on pages 134–135 in Impulsion.

HOW TO RIDE A FULL PIROUETTE
These aids apply to the full pirouette in walk and canter. The most important thing is to have a good quality collected walk or canter. Keep your horse in left or right position. To start the pirouette, half-halt and sit up tall, bracing the small of your back forwards and upwards towards your breastbone to lift the horse as he turns. Apply your outside leg behind the girth, asking the horse to turn, while keeping your inside leg down into the stirrup to anchor the pirouette on the spot as though turning around a dinner plate. Turn the horse with your hips and outside leg.

The inside rein asks the horse to turn, and the outside rein controls the speed of the turn. The smaller the pirouette, the firmer the inside rein needs to be, at the same time allowing the turn with the outside rein soft. Keep your chest in line with the horse's withers. Sit still! Your seat bones just need to allow the slight movement of the horse's back. See Rhythm page 31 for the horse's leg sequence in canter. To ride out of the pirouette, cease the aid to turn with your outside leg. Ask with your

Figures 6.9a–d *These four photographs show Amadeus in the stages of a full canter pirouette. a) Amadeus shows good engagement behind and you can clearly see the forehand lifting and turning and the hind legs maintaining the canter sequence. b) Coming back down to earth at the end of a canter stride. I could be sitting up straighter. c) Good lowering of the haunches in true Lipizzaner style, but I am leaning forwards slightly, though this does not seem to have affected Amadeus (he could probably do just as well on his own!). d) A good finish to the pirouette with horse and rider in balance and ready to go forwards in canter.*

inside leg at the girth for the horse to step into the outside rein. Soften the inside rein. You should now be back into right or left position and ready to ride forwards again. (See Figures 6.9a–d)

THE EXERCISE
Firstly loosen the horse with stretching exercises. This exercise using demi-pirouettes and spirals can be ridden in walk and canter. Stretch the horse when changing the rein and afterwards.

Exercise 3a
Starting on the right rein in collected walk, ride as though on a four-loop serpentine, leaving the track just before V and heading to the centre line. As you reach the centre line, ride a demi walk pirouette to the right, and return to the track where you left it. Continue down the long side, maintaining right position, and turn across the school at E, riding a second demi-pirouette at X. Return to the track, proceed along it, turn across to the

centre line just after S. Ride a third demi-pirouette as you reach the centre line. Return to the track, and continue to C to finish the exercise. Repeat on the other rein in walk. Repeat on both reins in collected canter. (See Diagram 33a)

Exercise 3b

In Diagram 33b this next exercise is being ridden on the left rein. Ride a 15m circle with its centre point on the centre line. This can be anywhere on the centre line provided you have room to ride the circle, i.e. not too close to the short sides. Spiral inwards on the circle, maintaining left (inside) position. When the volte is as small as you can make it, apply the aids for a pirouette. You could ride a large pirouette at first, gradually decreasing the size until it is about the size of a dinner plate. Ride out of the pirouette (see pages 191–192) and resume the 15m circle. Before riding this exercise on the other rein, ride some trot exercises to refresh the horse and stretch him for a few minutes so that he is relaxed.

WHAT TO LOOK FOR

The canter and the walk must be good quality; the rhythm must be regular; the horse must be straight and listening to your aids. He should return to the track at the same place he left it. Collection requires a responsive horse and so he must be on your aids and not against the hand in any way. Make sure he is positioned properly to the right or left before you ask for demi- or full pirouettes. When riding exercise 3a, the horse must be positioned on a straight line across the centre of the school before asking for the demi-pirouette. When riding exercise 3b the horse must be straight on the circle as you spiral in. His haunches must not swing in or out. Spiralling in can be ridden as haunches-in, but the rider must take care that the haunches are not 'in' in the pirouette, otherwise it is not a true pirouette.

TRAINING TIPS

- Refresh the gait by riding working and medium trot to keep the horse thinking forwards.
- The more collected the horse, the more upright and supportive you

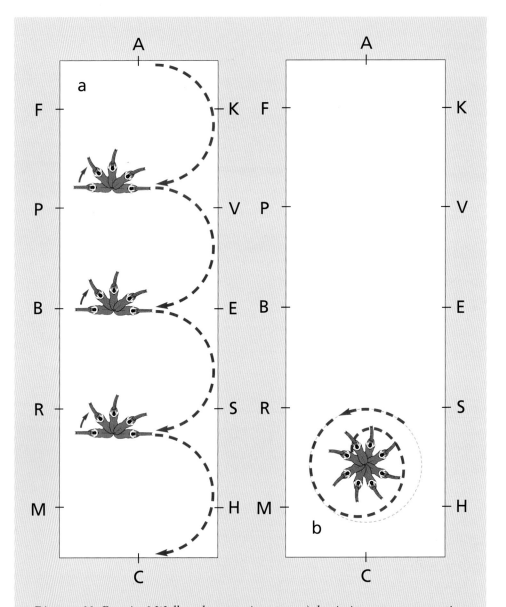

Diagram 33 *Exercise 3 Walk and canter pirouettes: a) demi-pirouettes on serpentine loops and b) spirals ridden into full pirouettes.*

should be with your back and stomach but the movement of your seat bones must be more subtle. The horse's back muscles lift under the saddle, which you must allow by being light in the saddle, but as the steps of the hind legs are small and carrying rather than big and driving you will not feel a lot going on underneath you. Many riders start pushing and shoving with the seat because they feel they should be doing something. What they *should* be doing is letting the horse get on with it!

- Exercise 3a can be ridden with full pirouettes on the centre line
- Exercise 3b can be ridden with a demi-pirouette before riding out again on the circle.

PROBLEM SOLVING

- If your pirouettes are too big and drift off the centre line, you will not return to the track where you left it. When you reach the track, repeat the demi-pirouette in the same direction as you are already travelling, and then return to the centre line and repeat again. You may need to do this a few times to improve the collection and accuracy of the demi-pirouettes.
- If you lean to the inside, the pirouette will no longer be a pirouette, but a spin on the inside foreleg. Sit up as tall as you can, keeping your shoulders level. If your inside shoulder drops, then you are leaning in. A spin is also caused by using too much inside rein.
- When riding canter pirouettes, if your horse changes legs behind as you exit the pirouette make sure you are sitting still, and maintain the canter lead with your outside leg behind the girth. Use your inside leg at the girth to ride the horse forwards in collected canter and spiral out on the circle, keeping him balanced.
- If the horse is on his forehand, he will not be able to turn around his haunches. Spend some time working on transitions and half-halts to improve his balance and establish self-carriage.

Exercise 4 (dressage)
Shortening the steps (collecting the stride)
AIM
This exercise helps with preparatory work for piaffe and passage. For these two movements to be performed correctly the horse must be strong enough in his back muscles to tuck his loins, and flex the joints of the hind legs so that he appears to be 'sitting' behind with the hind legs taking a great deal of weight.

SHORTENING THE TROT STEPS (COLLECTING THE STRIDE) IN PREPARATION FOR PIAFFE AND PASSAGE

In preparation for both piaffe and passage you need to practise shortening the trot steps, which have to be shorter and higher than in a normal collected trot, i.e. extra-collected. To collect the stride, a smaller trot movement is required from the seat bones. You must sit as tall and upright as possible, firming up the tone of the core – back and stomach – muscles in order to 'press with the back' (*Kreuz anziehen*), and close your legs onto the horse to hold the gait so that the steps cover less ground but become more elevated. You are, in effect, performing a series of half-halts. I often describe this feeling as 'picking the horse up around the middle'. Your seat muscles must remain soft and put no extra pressure onto the horse's back, otherwise he cannot lift his back underneath you. In other words, if you press down on the saddle, the horse cannot tuck his pelvis under and lift his loins, and does not therefore take weight behind, a necessary function of collection. Your legs should press downwards onto the stirrups to anchor the steps on the spot more and inhibit forwards motion.

To release the horse from the shortened trot, soften your holding aids – legs and back – to allow the horse to go forwards again and start to do a bigger trot with your seat bones, with your back swinging with the horse's back. The rein contact should be as soft as possible at all times. If you have given the aids correctly with the whole body, you should be able to do an extra-collected trot on loose reins; the horse must not be shortened and held tightly by the reins alone.

PIAFFE

See page 183 for the aids to piaffe.

Shortening the walk steps (collecting the stride)

Piaffe can be developed from an extra-collected walk. It is most important that your horse has a good walk and is able to keep the walk steps in rhythm in extreme collection. Piaffe evolves naturally from a very collected walk as a release of bottled-up energy, or impulsion. As the walk has no moment of suspension, the energy generated becomes cadenced steps in piaffe, where there is a moment of suspension between each diagonal pair of legs being in contact with the ground.

To give the walk extra collection, you need to pick the horse up around the middle as described above, do a smaller walk motion with your seat bones, and sit up tall and upright in the saddle. Use half-halts to bring the horse into the desired amount of collection. Press your legs downwards into the stirrups, as with shortening the trot, to anchor the walk. The rein contact should be as soft as possible with the horse not being held by the reins but accepting the contact and softening the jaw (quietly chewing). The rider should be able to release the rein contact altogether if the horse is truly balanced.

Piaffe can also be developed from collected trot by preparing for a walk transition but going into extra-collected trot for a few steps before actually walking.

PASSAGE

See page 184 for the aids to passage.

Releasing the energy

The passage is a release for the horse's energy when collecting his medium trot, resulting in the springy, lofty passage steps. The energy has to go somewhere and as he cannot go forwards so much, he springs higher off the ground. From passage you can shorten the steps into piaffe, which helps to keep impulsion in piaffe. On the contrary, from piaffe you can lengthen the steps into passage, which helps to keep the elevation in the passage.

THE EXERCISE

Loosen your horse up on a long rein in all three gaits. Prepare him for this exercise with lots of transitions between collected and extended walk and trot, and trot to halt transitions. Use canter work on a circle to either give the horse a break or for relaxation at the end of the training session.

Exercise 4a piaffe

Work in half the school on the track, turning across from E to B or B to E depending on which rein you are on. Using straight lines will help you to keep the horse straight. At each letter around the half of the arena alternate between collected walk, and extra-collected walk. Ride this on each rein and then ride the same pattern alternating collected trot with extra-collected trot. During the extra-collected steps, ask for a few steps of piaffe. (See Diagram 34a)

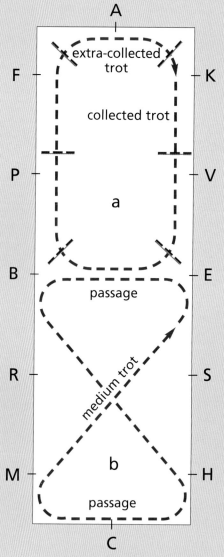

Exercise 4b passage

Using half the arena, ride collected medium trot on the short sides and normal medium trot on the short diagonals between M and E and B and H. On the short sides of the school, ask for a few steps of passage during the collected medium trot steps. Ride this on both reins. (See Diagram 34b)

Diagram 34 Exercise 4 *Shortening the trot steps. Transitions within the gait from extra-collected to collected and back to collected, working in half the school as a rectangle with straight lines and corners. In the other half of the school, passage is ridden across the short side and across the middle of the school, and medium trot on the short diagonals. a) shortening the trot steps to work towards piaffe; b) shortening medium trot steps to work towards passage.*

WHAT TO LOOK FOR

As you ride the different exercises, the rhythm must be regular, and there should be no speeding up and slowing down of the tempo. Piaffe and passage steps may be slower at first as the horse becomes accustomed to the 'sitting down' in piaffe, and the loftier steps and the increase in cadence of passage. You should aim to maintain the same tempo as collected trot. A well-balanced horse should be able to piaffe and passage at the same tempo of the collected trot, providing the trot is not too fast of course!

TRAINING TIPS

- Ride medium trot frequently to release excess tension so that your horse does not become tight in the back, stressed or boil over.
- Too much bracing of the back and a tight contact turns piaffe into levade; you may get airs above the ground that you were not expecting! The horse must be in front of your leg at all times.
- The rein contact must be soft to allow the hind legs to step forward under the body; Firm reins block the trot motion of both piaffe and passage and the steps will become irregular (loss of rhythm).
- Working alongside the wall or fence in position will help to keep the horse straight. A line of poles across the EB line of the arena will give an extra straight line to ride along.

PROBLEM SOLVING

- If you ride piaffe from the walk, without ensuring that the walk is a good collected walk and relaxed, the horse may become tense. This can lead to restlessness in the halt, rearing, spinning around or running backwards. Make sure you can halt correctly after piaffe with the horse relaxed. If the horse is too tense to listen to your aids, then do something simpler! Resume the exercise another day.
- If the horse cannot stay straight, and swings his haunches from side to side, use lateral work to make him looser (more supple), especially shoulder-in. Make sure you can ride the horse in position on circles and straight lines (see Straightness, page 147).

- If the horse runs away from passage against the reins, then spend some time riding transitions. A horse can run away if he is tense and tightens his back. Interspersing canter work with this exercise, therefore, will ensure the back muscles relax because the back works differently in a canter stride than it does in a trot stride as the canter is a one-sided movement and not a diagonal movement.

Exercise 5 (jumping)
Demi-pirouettes into jumps
AIM

The aim of this exercise is to improve collection before approaching an obstacle by riding demi-pirouettes in the canter. These 'short turns' when ridden close to a fence are invaluable in knocking seconds of your time in a jump-off. Being able to turn on a sixpence enables you to do a fast round without actually speeding up.

THE EXERCISE

Place two jumps one in the middle of each long side. Construct them so that they can both be jumped from the right and left rein. One should be an upright and the other a parallel. The jumps should be between 0.5m (1ft 6in) and 1m (3ft) high. The parallel should be as wide as it is high. Loosen the horse up on a long rein in walk, trot and canter on both reins, and then ride transitions on the bit especially walk–canter–walk to improve the engagement of the hind legs. Collected canter must then be established.

Exercise 4a
On the right rein, in right-lead canter, approach fence 1, the upright. Continue straight on after the fence, maintaining right position. Collect the canter until it is almost on the spot and ride a demi-pirouette in the canter in the corner. Approach the jump again with a flying change of lead to left canter three or four steps away from the fence. Jump the fence again. Continue straight on, ride a demi-pirouette to the left in the corner, continue in left canter towards the fence, ride a flying

change three or four steps away from the fence into right-lead canter, and jump again. This can be repeated over fence 2, the parallel. (See Diagram 35a)

Exercise 4b

On the left rein, in left-lead canter, approach fence 2 in collected canter. After the jump, continue in left lead. Ride a demi-pirouette left in the corner, approach the jump again still in left lead. Jump the fence, ride another demi-pirouette to the left in the corner, and approach the jump again. Repeat two or three times over the same jump. This exercise can be done over both fences and should be ridden on both reins. (See Diagram 35b)

WHAT TO LOOK FOR

The horse must be straight every time on the approach and after the fence. The demi-pirouettes should be in line with the middle of each fence. If riding flying changes before the fence, they must also be straight so the horse can keep sufficient collection (weight behind) to jump with impulsion. (See Figures 6.10a and b).

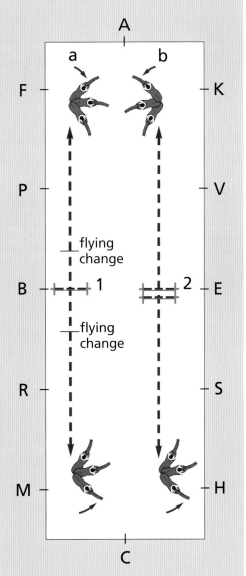

Diagram 35 *Exercise 5 Using demi-pirouettes to improve collection between jumps. a) with a change of lead; b) without a change of lead.*

Figures 6.10a and b *Collection, or the ability to take weight behind, before a fence. a) (above left) A collected horse will jump with impulsion from his haunches. The rider will be able to place the horse accurately at the fence for take-off. b) (above right) Collection applies just as much to the event horse, not just when jumping but also when travelling over uneven ground between fences; this horse is both balanced and collected.*

TRAINING TIPS

- Pairs of cones placed either side of each fence can help you to stay straight, for the changes of lead in particular.
- When staying on the same canter lead for the demi-pirouettes, make sure you do not wander off the line. Straightness is crucial to collection. The horse should 'sit' in the demi-pirouettes.
- If the horse becomes too excited in the demi-pirouettes and tries to speed up towards the fence, keep the horse on your aids by varying the pirouettes, riding full or double pirouettes instead. Then resume the demi-pirouettes.

PROBLEM SOLVING

- If you come in too fast to the fence, your flying change will most likely be unsuccessful, with the horse changing late behind, which will not help on take-off, and he will be unbalanced. If you have problems with the changes, ride a simple change before the fence instead to give the horse confidence.

- If your demi-pirouettes are not successful, ride them a bit larger to keep the forwardness of the canter, and decrease the size of the demi-pirouettes each time until the hind legs are covering an area the size of a dinner plate.
- If your horse has difficulty changing lead so close to the fence, do it a few more strides away. It is better to ensure the quality of the change than jump the fence disunited. You can then change a little closer each time.

Exercise 6 (jumping)
Using lateral work between jumps
AIM

The aim of this exercise is to use lateral movements to help you to place your horse really accurately into fences. Riding specific lateral movements to alter the line of approach keeps the horse collected and in balance, whereas veering off line and making an emergency pull on the inside rein will unbalance the horse and disturb his balance before take-off or after the fence.

THE EXERCISE

Place two jumps in the arena, one halfway down each long side. As with the previous exercise, one should be a parallel and one an upright, which allows both these jumping exercises to be practised in the same session without having to alter the fences. Loosen the horse on a long rein in all three gaits. Ride transitions on the bit, and lateral movements such as shoulder-in, leg-yield, and half-pass. The jumps can be approached from trot or canter.

On the left rein, establish counter-canter (right lead) making sure the horse is in right position before the corner at H (counter-flexion). Ride leg-yield to the left across the short diagonal (to B) to the take-off point for fence 1, the upright. Jump the fence, then ride straight for a few steps before riding a half-circle to the right to the take-off point for fence 2. (See Diagram 36a) Jump fence 2 and then change the rein on the short diagonal towards M staying in right-lead canter. (See Diagram 36b) Repeat the exercise two or three times. Then, on the right rein, establish right-lead canter at A. Ride half-pass to the right across the short diagonal KB. Jump fence 1 and change canter lead to the left near R. Ride a half circle to the take-off point for fence 2. (See Diagram 36c) Jump fence 2 and then change the rein on the short diagonal towards F. Change canter lead to the right. (See Diagram 36d) Repeat the exercise two or three times.

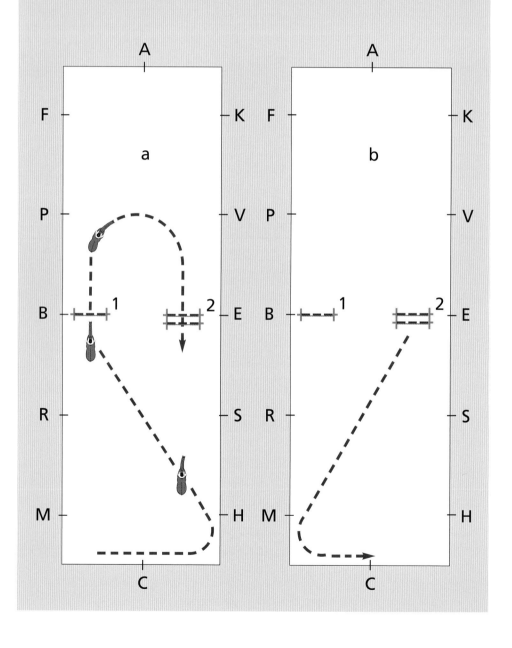

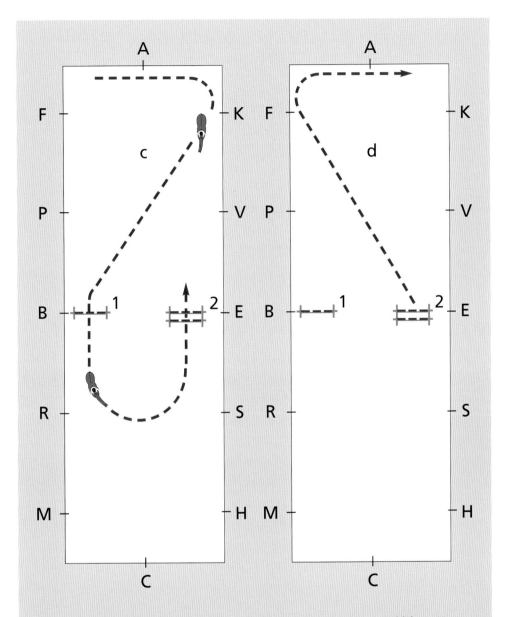

Diagram 36 *Exercise 6 using lateral work between jumps. a) Leg-yield from H to fence 1. Jump the fence and then ride a half circle to the take-off point for fence 2. b) Jump the fence and then change the rein on the short diagonal towards M without changing canter lead and repeat the exercise two or three times, and then try it on the other rein. c) On the right rein, ride half-pass right from K to fence 1. Jump the fence and change canter lead to the left before riding a half circle to the take-off point for fence 2. d) Jump the fence and change the rein on the short diagonal towards F with a change of lead at F to right-lead canter. Repeat the exercise two or three times, and then try it on the other rein.*

WHAT TO LOOK FOR

You should always aim to end your lateral movement in line with the centre of the fence you are approaching. Make sure your horse is always straight for take-off so that he can push off from both hind feet. Ensure your lateral movements are correctly executed; letting your horse fall out through his outside shoulder and drift sideways is not a leg-yield, which will only unbalance him and your take-off will not be straight. The idea of using lateral movements is to improve flexibility and obedience to the aids so that you can place your horse accurately to the fence. Prepare for lateral movements by riding accurate turns and corners, which will position the horse for whatever movement you are riding. Counter-flexion through corners is necessary to set the horse up for the leg-yield exercise below.

TRAINING TIPS

- This exercise also works well riding half-pass to the fences. On the right rein, keep the horse to inside position (left) on the corner at H. Ride half-pass left to fence 1. Jump the fence, continue straight in left canter. Change lead on the short side to right canter. Repeat on the other rein.
- Practise working in counter-canter and true canter around the school, changing lead every few steps. This also helps with preparation for tempi-changes.
- Ride leg-yield in canter as well as in trot on a regular basis so that your horse moves easily away from your inside leg at the girth. (**Note** This is why in leg-yield the inside leg should always be *at* the girth, and not *behind* the girth. Otherwise your horse will change leg, or break into trot.)

PROBLEM-SOLVING

- If your horse does become disunited in canter leg-yield, make sure your inside leg stays at the girth when you use it. May riders swing their inside leg back when applying an aid. Also, make sure his neck is not pulled to the inside with a strong inside rein. He must work from your inside leg to your outside hand.

- If your horse travels too much sideways in the leg-yield towards the fence, ride a small circle of 8–10m in diameter as you reach the centre line. Ride the circle in the same direction as the horse is facing, i.e. if he is bending right, circle to the right. Continue in leg-yield to the fence as before.
- If your horse does not travel sideways enough to reach the line of approach, circle away in the direction he is facing, and start again. You may need to take a break from the jumping exercise and work on leg-yielding on a circle so that the horse is more responsive to your inside leg/outside rein aids.

Conclusion

Working through this book, it should become obvious that the scales of training all interlink. At all levels of training, a horse should be worked with some degree of each scale. With the novice horse, the first three scales Rhythm, Suppleness (Looseness) and Contact are most important, but you cannot ignore the other three scales, Impulsion, Straightness and Collection, and leave them until later on. There is no point in just concentrating on Rhythm alone and disregarding the fact that your horse is crooked and leaning on the reins!

If you hit a problem and your horse does not understand what you are asking, always take a step back in his training, working on earlier exercises until he is ready to progress again. A novice horse who is not straight, for example, will not work in a rhythm. Without any collection, or taking weight behind, the young horse will be on his forehand and lean on the reins, i.e. he will not be able to accept the contact. A novice horse who cannot go forwards from the rider's aids, i.e. has no impulsion, will not develop suppleness through his back.

The scales develop in layers; every time the horse reaches a higher level of training, the scales must be reassessed and improved. For example, a horse doing piaffe requires perfection in all the scales at the same time, and riding tempi-changes demands great skill from the rider in keeping the horse absolutely straight, in rhythm, and with great impulsion.

I hope you find this book a useful addition to your bookshelf; one that you can refer to time and time again as you progress with your horse!

Index